Self-Help?
Self-Hypnosis!

Zetta Thomelin

Grosvenor House
Publishing Limited

All rights reserved
Copyright © Zetta Thomelin, 2020

First Edition

Zetta Thomelin asserts the moral right to be identified as the
author of this work.

The right of Zetta Thomelin to be identified as the author of this
work has been asserted in accordance with Section 78
of the Copyright, Designs and Patents Act 1988

The book cover is copyright to Zetta Thomelin
Cover photo copyright to Jule Messingschlager
Back cover author photo copyright to John Christian Jacques

This book is published by
Grosvenor House Publishing Ltd
Link House
140 The Broadway, Tolworth, Surrey, KT6 7HT.
www.grosvenorhousepublishing.co.uk

This book is sold subject to the conditions that it shall not, by way of
trade or otherwise, be lent, resold, hired out or otherwise circulated
without the author's or publisher's prior consent in any form of binding or
cover other than that in which it is published and
without a similar condition including this condition being imposed
on the subsequent purchaser.

All rights reserved. No part of this publication may be reproduced, stored in a
retrieval system, or transmitted, in any form or by any means, electronic,
mechanical, photocopying, recording or otherwise, without the prior written
permission of the author.

The author can be contacted at www.headtogether.net

A CIP record for this book
is available from the British Library

ISBN 978-1-83975-053-3

Dedicated to the memory of my father Paul Thomelin, who encouraged me in all my endeavours.

With thanks to Evelyn Meyer and Barbara Thomelin for their patient proof reading and their support.

Also by Zetta Thomelin

Books
The Healing Metaphor – Hypnotherapy Scripts

Audio
Journeys into Nature
Avebury and Silbury Hill
Sleep
Relieve Stress

Contents

About this book xi
Introduction xi

Does Hypnosis work? 1
Case study Enhanced Learning 1
Case study Sleep walking 3
Case study Anxiety 3
Case study Grief 5
Case study Insomnia 7

What is Hypnosis? 9
The Trance State 9

How the mind works 11
Conscious 11
Subconscious 11
Unconscious 12
Critical faculty 13
Brain wave states 14
What if I fall asleep? 16

Resistance 18

The Power of suggestion 19
What is suggestion? 19
The Placebo 20
The Nocebo 21
Testing your response to suggestion 22

The mind body relationship 27
The Stress Response 27

How to get into trance 30
Cue Words 30
Eye Closure 31
Wipers..32
Numbers 33
Hot Air Balloon 34
Body scan...35
Self-Hypnosis outdoors 36

Coming out of Trance 38
Will I wake up? 38
How to come of trance...38

What to do in trance 40
Direct suggestions 40
Indirect suggestions 41
Metaphors..43
Affirmations 46
Future Pacing 46

Planning your self-hypnosis session 48
Non recorded session 48
Recorded session 49

Areas of Treatment:...50
Addiction 50
About Addiction 50
Cutting the connection to addiction 51
Alcohol 53
Smoking 55
Gambling 56
Food...58

CONTENTS

Anger 63
About anger 63
Visualisation 65
Direct suggestions for anger 66
Indirect suggestions for anger 66
Metaphor Fanning the Flames 66
Affirmations 67

Anxiety 68
About Anxiety 68
Direct suggestions for Anxiety 70
Indirect suggestions for Anxiety 70
Metaphor   Spinning Top 71
                       Dials 71
                       Spam Filter 72
Affirmations 73

Confidence 74
About Confidence 74
Social media and confidence 75
Modelling 76
Modelling for confidence 76
Law of Association and Anchoring 77
How to use hypnotic anchoring 78
Challenging your beliefs about yourself - Reality Check 79
Self-Appreciation 82
Metaphor   Tennis Court 83
                       Fairground Mirror 84
Affirmations 85

Depression 86
About Depression 86
Direct suggestions for depression 87

Indirect suggestions for depression 88
Metaphor   Retune the Mind 88
        The Weaver...89
        The Mind, A Screen 90
Affirmations 91

Grief 92
About Grief 92
Metaphor, Bereavement, The Receiver 94
Cutting the connection to past relationship 95
Metaphor, old relationship, rose-tinted spectacles 96
Direct suggestions for grief 97
Indirect suggestions for grief 98
Affirmations 98

Insomnia 99
About Insomnia 99
Bi-Modal sleep pattern 99
Circadian rhythms 100
Sleep Misperception 100
Insomnia Causes 101
Sleep Trigger 102
Law of Reverse Effect 103
Strategies to use in conjunction with Self-Hypnosis 104
Direct suggestions for Insomnia 105
Indirect suggestions for Insomnia 105
Metaphor with sleep trigger 105
Metaphor The Bag 106
Affirmations 107

Pain 108
About Pain 108
Direct suggestions for Pain 110

CONTENTS

Indirect suggestions for Pain 110
Metaphor   Red ball 111
        Pain control system 112
Affirmations 113

Patience 114
About Patience 114
Direct Suggestions for Patience 114
Indirect Suggestions for Patience 115
Metaphor The Kettle 115

Performance Enhancement 116
Improving performance 116
Direct suggestion   Sport 116
        Exams 117
        Enhancing Memory 117
Positive Resource for exams 118
Rehearsal technique for exams 119
Rehearsal technique for improved physical performance 120
Affirmations 121

Phobia 122
About Phobia 122
Direct Suggestions for Phobia 123
Indirect Suggestions for Phobia 123
Cinema technique 123
Affirmations 126

Physical conditions 127
IBS 127
Hot flushes 130
Immune System 132
Anorgasmia 134
Skin complaints 137

Nausea 138
Trust your body 140

Resilience 141
What is resilience 141
Story telling... 143
Example session one Story telling.. 145
Example session two Story telling....................................... 148

Sample sessions 151
Cue words session for confidence 151
Sample session for overthinking 152
Complex recorded session for anger 155

About this book

Introduction

There is a huge amount of mystique surrounding self-hypnosis, even more than around hypnosis itself. In this book I want to dispel the myths and show you how easy it can be to access the trance state by yourself, you are in fact often doing so without realising it, so you will be able to harness the potential it grants you for change. Many of the books about self-hypnosis spend a lot of time explaining the trance state and how to get yourself into trance, but do not give you much help on what to do when you get there, mostly giving just simple affirmations which would be as useful in or outside of trance. I wanted to provide something far more useful, that takes you beyond understanding trance, into how to really impact on your own subconscious and make changes for yourself. With the help of this book, you will be able to plan your own treatment programme and understand the different ways you can utilise therapy in hypnosis. Even the process of planning your sessions becomes a part of your therapy itself.

Self-help is important because it is empowering, we are not relying on others to provide the answers, but looking within to create the change that we need. As a hypnotherapist I am keen for my clients to become self-actualising and take control of their road to change. One way they can do this and indeed anyone can do this, is to utilise the power of self-hypnosis. Creating your own therapy is self-affirming, as it can also be tailored to you in a very targeted way, as nobody knows your needs as clearly as you do, you cannot so easily cheat yourself as you can someone else, you can look inside and find the real answer to your own needs without an intermediary giving you their interpretation.

Self-hypnosis is even more useful now with the advances of modern technology, almost everyone has a recording device on their phone, so they can have their own therapy on the go, made easier by the audio prompts.

This book is divided into clear sections so you can understand about the hypnotic trance, how it will help you access your subconscious mind, utilise the power of suggestion and take greater control of your stress response. It is then broken into specific areas with which you might need help, giving a variety of approaches that you can use. The modern world is so stressful, especially in times of economic strain, relationships suffer as do aspirations. The result can be psychological issues such as anxiety, anger, addictions, grief, depression, but also physical issues resulting from the strain on the body from being in perpetual fight or flight mode, such as migraines, IBS and pain, ideas to work with all of these areas are detailed in this book.

If you want further ideas to use once you have mastered self-hypnosis, then you can look at my book "The Healing Metaphor" which contains a rich source of new metaphors.

Does Hypnosis work?

Self-Hypnosis and Hypnotherapy use the combination of hypnosis and therapeutic work, therefore are very different to stage hypnosis, where the trance state is being used to entertain. When using self-hypnosis, you are putting yourself into trance to do something therapeutically to help yourself. Your first question may well be "Does it work?" Most people are familiar with hypnotherapy for stopping smoking and perhaps for phobias like fear of flying, but it can be used for a range of conditions and so I wanted to present at the beginning of the book a few case studies to show how it can be used and the results it can get, before you start work on helping yourself, understanding just how much you can achieve will help you to commit to the process. Some of the cases I am sharing with you use self-hypnosis and some involve hypnosis with someone else, but they have supported their work with self-hypnosis, you can equally achieve change by yourself if you want that change, as working with someone else. Reading through these case studies will help you to get ideas to help yourself as well as showing how helpful hypnosis can be.

Case Study Enhanced Learning and Exams using Self-Hypnosis

A 40-year-old woman had an exam in two weeks, she was struggling to remember things and had low confidence about passing. Her tutor had said she might not be ready to take the exam which accelerated her decline in confidence, but she wanted to try to take it as she could always retake if she failed, she wanted to set herself the goal of trying her best to pass. She did just two fully planned sessions for herself.

She knew that the stress response could cloud her thinking, as blood flow is diverted from the forebrain to the hind brain, so one of the keys to remembering and thinking clearly in an exam, is to remain relaxed. With this in mind, she created a positive resource (you will find information on this in the confidence section) that would relax her before going into the exam or if she began to get stressed during the exam. She visualised within trance all the doubt leaving her mind, like thought bubbles leaving her mind and going into a cloud, a cloud that the sun would burn away. She visualised her success in the exam and receiving her certificate when she had passed, we call this future pacing. She used a script about breaking conditioning, which focuses on how elephants are trained. What they do is to tie the elephant when it is very young to a tree, so that it learns that the sensation of the rope means it has to stay still, when they are fully grown and could pull that tree right out by the roots, they still just stand there as they believe they cannot go anywhere even though they could if they tried, it is just conditioning. So, she challenged her conditioned response that she could not remember and expected to fail, she worked on the conditioned response of expecting to pass rather than to fail, seeing there was a choice of focus.

She felt more in control and was remembering things better but in a mock test she had still made some mistakes. Her tutor was giving her some extra coaching, but was still offering her the opportunity to pull out of the exam, which was sending out negative signals of failure to her. She was determined to take it anyway. The words that kept coming back to her were the story of the conditioned elephant who could have broken free, this seemed to have a powerful impact for her.

In the second session she planned for herself, she looked at the idea of how differently people react to a journey, some with anxiety, some with enjoyment and used it to lock into the opportunity ahead of her that the exam posed, the opportunity to succeed. She built in suggestions that she would begin to remember times when she had succeeded at job interviews, exams, winning friends etc., allowing the feeling of success to bubble up to the surface, like bubbles of air coming up through water. She found different ways to release her doubts and built in some direct suggestions around things she specifically needed to remember for the exam. She recorded both sessions for herself and listened to them regularly up to the exam. She passed the exam, surprising her tutor, but not herself and she felt she had resolved some other issues along the way.

Case Study for Sleep Walking using Self-Hypnosis

A woman of 45 had been very unwell and after she recovered found she was sleep walking at night, it was rather like night-terrors, she would jump up and run around, as if she were in danger. This was caused by fear in the subconscious created by the illness, it had not caught up with the fact that the danger had passed.

She worked with a very simple form of self-hypnosis using cue words and relaxation. She had chosen the cue word "bluebell" as she loved the flowers and could visualise bluebells in a wood as she started her work, so she said the word and then worked through a simple body relaxation when in bed and preparing to sleep, she then said "bluebell" a second time and then repeated to herself the simple phrase "I will not sleep walk", she would repeat this like a mantra about 10 times, sometimes more, then end the session by repeating her cue word again. She would then settle down to sleep.

After three nights of repeating this process the sleep walking stopped, she carried on for two more nights just to be sure. The sleep walking stayed away for two years, then she was under some stress and it happened again one night, so she went back to her routine and after a couple of nights it stopped again. She resolved to repeat the process just once a month to keep the sleep walking at bay and this has worked well for her. So, as you can see the sessions do not always need to be complex.

Case Study for Anxiety using Hypnotherapy

A young woman came to see me to get help while on long term sick leave for anxiety and depression, due to being bullied by a colleague at work. Her home life was stable, she was happy with her partner and had three children, but this heightened state of anxiety was causing her to frequently snap at her family. Her GP had prescribed anti-depressants and she was signed off work. When she came to see me, she was in discussions with her employer about returning to work, the thought of returning had increased her anxiety to unmanageable levels and on top of that she found herself unable to read her emails for fear of what news they may contain. She wanted to be able to stand up for herself and to be able to deal with things (like the emails) without getting herself into a state of panic.

I asked her to complete a short questionnaire that assesses depression and anxiety (Hamilton Anxiety Rating Scale HAM-D), her score extremely high, showing her anxiety levels to be more than severe. My main priority was to help her deal with the bullying, partly by building her confidence, but I also wanted to help her relax as much as possible and learn how to manage the panic attacks.

I started with a slow induction, followed by a deepener and then worked on helping relax even further by using a mindfulness body scan. This helped her into a nice relaxed state. I then created for her a positive resource (an anchor to recall a powerful positive emotion at will) something she could use at any time when she felt her anxiety rising. This was followed by visualisation to help her reduce her worries and negative thoughts and some direct suggestions to help her understand that no matter how bad they might feel panic attacks will not cause her harm. I finished the session with a metaphor visualising a control panel in her mind to help her take control of her anxiety and turn it down (having initially discussed how her stress response works) by turning the levels down, she was reducing the flood of her system with stress chemicals. I gave her some simple self-hypnosis to do at home, using cue words and direct suggestions, to build her confidence and asked to her try and take time out to go to the gym, something she had previously told me she really enjoyed.

After the first session she told me that she had started dealing with the emails she had not been able to read before and she was back at work. The bully had been sacked and things were generally going well. I started the second session by asking her to complete the same questionnaire and her score had reduced significantly but still showed some anxiety.

After inducing a trance state, I worked on helping her let go of worries using direct suggestion to explain that worrying is predicting the future with a negative outcome. I followed this with another control room metaphor and a couple of stories, all designed to give her the ability to let go of such worries and not let them bother her. I also got her to use a modelling technique to get her to see herself dealing with things successfully, in a way someone she respected and admired would do. We did another couple of sessions to look at how it was that she allowed people to bully her, she examined her past and in trance stood up to various people through visualisation that had bullied her before, and she found this very empowering. We also utilised a technique often referred to as cutting the ties, which enables the cutting of emotional impact someone can have on you, enabling her to cut off from the bullies emotionally and a self-appreciation technique to build up her self-esteem, all these techniques are detailed further on in the book. When we did a follow up the anxiety score was now at a negligible level. She gradually came off her medication under supervision and kept using the self-hypnosis techniques she had learned.

Case Study – Grief using Hypnotherapy

A woman in her 50s, who had seen me previously for stress related issues, came to see me when her son died in tragic circumstances. She wanted to be able to attend the funeral and give the eulogy without breaking down, she felt this was something she wanted to do for him but felt she needed help to do so, as she was obviously distraught at the loss of her son. She also wanted to be strong for her other child who was trying to deal with their own loss, but worrying about their Mum too.

SELF-HELP? SELF-HYPNOSIS!

Things moved pretty quickly towards the funeral, so we booked a session on the morning of the funeral, as we had worked together before, she found it easy to slip into trance and I could see the relief in her features at being able to let go for a while and begin to drift down, leaving her troubled conscious mind behind. I then worked with a metaphor I often use with people who are dealing with grief, it is a metaphor that may be a familiar, one which compares the body to a radio receiving a transmission, the radio may no longer work but the transmission still exists, it is not an overtly religious metaphor, so most people can work with it and it helps them to feel some sense of connection with the person they have lost. I also try to work with a positive memory of the departed to try to move away from the focus of recent times. In some cases, if there are unresolved issues I will create a space where the person can have a conversation in their mind with their lost loved one and play out any issues there, this was not relevant in this case and would anyway have been too soon, some time needs to have passed to face such an exercise.

I wanted to work beyond the processing of the grief to give her some sense of security whilst she was speaking to those gathered for the funeral, public speaking is hard enough for many people but in circumstances like this can be quite a traumatic experience. I worked with a metaphor of a tree that has deep roots that anchors it, talking about the deep roots she had with her family and friends that would be there with her, I got her to imagine she could feel those deep roots anchoring and holding her there when she was speaking and that if she began to struggle to feel those roots stretching down even deeper to hold her steady like a tree in a storm, she was anchored and held safe there. I got her to imagine how the tree is nourished from its root system and to take nourishment from her root system. I wanted to give her a strong visual image she could hold onto and one that had some relationship to reality, as she did have a strong group of people around her, rooting for her and caring for her, I wanted her to feel that tangible support. We worked on some breathing exercises to calm her as well and revisited some of the work we had done for her strength before relating to her previous achievements and successes and noting that even when that flood of emotion comes, it will pass if you do not stoke it like a fire, to let it fizzle out perhaps until the time is right to deal with it.

She contacted me after the funeral and said she had managed to keep her composure during the funeral and felt she had done her son proud; she had worked with the roots image as she stood there and felt the work we had done had really strengthened her. She showed incredible courage in very difficult circumstances and went on to support those around her who were coping less well with their loss.

Case Study Insomnia using Self-Hypnosis

A 55-year-old man had chronic Insomnia aggravated by arthritis pain in his hands. He had not been sleeping for more than 3 hours a night for some time, following a visit to his GP, he was now taking sleeping tablets, they had steadily increased the dose and he was taking 7.5 mg a night, but the GP was saying this could not be a permanent solution to his sleep problems, especially as he was also taking strong pain relief. He was turning to self-hypnosis as a last hope. He needed to tackle this on two fronts, as without approaching the pain issues the sleep would not be resolved, though the sleep problems were not solely linked to the pain as he had done work in the past which required being on call, since when his sleep patterns had never been good.

In the first session he did for himself he created a positive resource state linked to a good memory to get him focusing on something positive, the long periods of sleeplessness and dependence on pills had really eroded his self-worth and led to focusing very much on the negatives in his life, which often happens with both chronic pain and insomnia. He introduced the idea of a sleep trigger telling himself that his subconscious was waiting for a signal to take over, it was just not getting the signal as his mind was over thinking, he told the subconscious the signal to look out for, he used the image of the sunset as he loved the sea and he used some suggestions about change and not anticipating things will stay the same. To help with the pain he utilised an idea that a therapist called Milton Erickson created when dealing with pain, which points out that we have an incredible ability to anesthetise our body, as we can lose the awareness of the sensation for example of our trousers on our legs, which we only notice if our attention is drawn to it, yet no anaesthetic was used, we just altered our focus and lost the sensation, this is true of all body sensations when the mind is very absorbed.

He created a second session, but he had already cut down to 1.5mg of his tablets over a two-week period and using the recording he had made every night. On the second session he worked with the concept that, the harder you try to sleep the more difficult it becomes, like trying to remember a name. Trying not to think about sleep is a difficult concept, so he worked with distraction techniques, as soon as you stop trying to sleep, that is when sleep will come, just like when you give up trying as it is nearly morning and you fall asleep, most of us have experienced this. He worked with the idea that the mind can feel overloaded at bedtime from all the activity of the day, like a computer with too many things happening at the same time and steadily he cleared his mind, by switching off the concerns one at a time. For the physical problems he worked with the ability to switch off awareness of pain as sportsmen do when they go through the pain barrier, then adding the idea of a control panel that can switch off that awareness. Lastly, he worked with the idea that a warning light had flipped on to let him know he had a problem in his hands with the arthritis and that now he had received that message the light could go off now. He recorded his second session too, he kept alternating between the recording and found that he was managing his sleep so much better now.

What is Hypnosis? The Trance State

In using self-hypnosis to help ourselves we are utilising two things, the trance state and the power of suggestion to create change for ourselves, to take control of our own ability, to quite literally change our minds. So, let us examine these elements. When people talk about hypnosis, they are simply referring to the trance state, a trance state is something each of us experiences every day; it is a completely natural state, one that happens at least twice a day. When you first wake up in the morning and you have not opened your eyes yet, you are just becoming conscious, you are aware of sound, such as perhaps birds singing outside but cannot quite bring yourself to open your eyes yet, you feel cosy and comfortable and unaffected by troubles and demands of your daily life, this is a trance state. When you are just drifting off to sleep at night, we feel the same, drowsy and comfortable we are still slightly conscious but unaffected by an active mind, this is a trance state.

We also drift into a trance state at different times during the day, less deep perhaps, but nonetheless a trance state. For example; when you have driven along the motorway and you suddenly realise that you have passed junction turn offs and had not noticed; you have finished all the washing up but do not remember doing it; when you are playing an instrument and it feels like the instrument is almost playing itself, you become so focused and that the outside world disappears; when you are doing something creative like painting or maybe even something active like dancing or repetitive exercise, in all these situations we can zone out and drift into a trance state. There is a kind of music labelled as trance, one that is repetitive and lulls you into a zone where nothing outside the experience matters and maybe this concept can help understand the trance. It is not necessary to be deeply relaxed to go into trance, it is about the focus of attention, it can become frustrating if we get hooked up on the idea of being relaxed as it is a hard thing to force, but we can alter the focus of our attention and this can take us into trance.

We are not looking within hypnosis to become fully unconscious, it is not about being "knocked out", sometimes people use the expression being "put under", but you are not going under anything, if you lose all conscious awareness completely during your self-hypnosis you have drifted into a light sleep. In this state your brain waves slow down into what is known as the alpha state, beta is alert, alpha is drowsy, calm, we reach this state when meditating or doing something creative, it is just a case of slowing down the mind, the electrical pulses that create the resonance in the mind. Following this are the theta and delta states when the brain waves have slowed down enough to allow sleep to occur, we will look at this in a bit more detail later.

In hypnotherapy we are coaching people into a trance state for a therapeutic purpose and in self-hypnosis you are doing exactly the same thing. When someone is in the trance state, we can access their subconscious mind and affect changes in behaviour, you can do this too, so long as it is change that you really want to achieve. When in a trance, the conscious mind has gone partly off duty, it is there but not in controlling mode. This is the way we can access the subconscious mind to affect a change, it is like the hard drive on your computer with a faulty programme that we need to work on and repair, or to use an older metaphor it is a pre-recorded tape that needs recording over. This can also be achieved through self-hypnosis, if you have the will to make a change then hypnosis can open the door to that change. To fully understand this, we need to look at the idea of the conscious and subconscious mind.

How the Mind Works

Conscious Mind

The mind and the divisions within are a matter of debate but, I am sure you have all come across the terms, conscious, subconscious and unconscious. The conscious, is that part of your mind engaged with this book and paying attention right now. It is the part of you that creates, concentrates with full awareness of what you are doing, in this state you are very aware also of your sense of self. The conscious mind is the part of the mind that turns those worries over and over and you may feel it is the part that makes choices, for example, about what you want to do with your day, what you want to eat, but many of our so-called conscious decisions are informed by what has happened in the past and that is held within the layer beneath.

Subconscious Mind

The subconscious mind is the layer beneath, some people simplify it by calling it the lower mind. This subconscious holds all our patterns of behaviour, it is like our computer hard drive it holds memories and learned tasks, like our ability to drive, walk, read and write, also most of our bodily functions are controlled by the subconscious mind. At first, when we learn for example to drive, we do it with total conscious focus, but through repetition it sinks into the subconscious and the conscious mind no longer has to give the task so much of the attention. The subconscious holds your learnings, your conscious mind learned all those letters when you learned to read, but then your subconscious took over, it is recognising and interpreting the letters on the page and giving the ideas to your conscious mind to process and think about. Of course, not all our learning experiences are positive ones, our bad habits and addictions are locked in there and also our fears. If you were bitten by a dog as a child, it may well leave you with a deep seated fear of dogs that comes into force whenever you see one, you do not actively, consciously think about it, but your subconscious having seen the dog might send you straight into "fight or flight" mode, because it remembers what happened before and it wants to protect you from it happening again. It does not process the fact that you have encountered dogs many times since this one bad experience and been just fine, it is locked into a learned fear of dogs. The information stored in the subconscious could be described like bubbles coming up through water, information bubbles up from the subconscious into the conscious mind as a thought form or as an active behaviour.

It is generally believed now that only 10 per cent of what we do each day is controlled by conscious mind, we feel our conscious mind is making the decisions and controlling our lives, but it is not.

Unconscious Mind

The Unconscious was defined by Jung as the layer beneath the subconscious and he believed that the unconscious communicated with the conscious mind through the subconscious, it acted like the middle-man in the communication between the three parts of the mind. Jung believed that there was additionally something he called the collective unconscious, which was like a well of information that all people can access, it is not limited to the individual, it is out there in the ether somewhere and we can all tap into it. He uses this idea to explain how things like scientific discoveries can be made simultaneously in different places, or how societies that had no means of communication can have the same kinds of symbolism, they are all accessing this collective vat of information. Freud saw the Unconscious somewhat differently, as the place where we store socially unacceptable ideas, feelings and thoughts, the things we barely like to acknowledge, that we feel that might contradict accepted social norms and also more traumatic experiences, should we have had any such experiences.

Some believe that the subconscious and unconscious is in fact the same thing and often therapists will interchange both terms.

Whatever your interpretation of the two lower layers beneath our conscious awareness, the most important fact is that we can affect change to the patterns and beliefs locked in the area of the mind below the conscious. It is hard when fully conscious to get directly into the layer beneath, to gain communication from the top down, the information is usually travelling from the lower layer upwards. The easiest way to directly affect change is through the trance state, hypnosis.

Critical faculty

It is generally accepted now, that up until the age of about five we accept everything that is going on around us without question, we learn our information about the world around us from our immediate environment and we have not yet developed the truly conscious sense of a questioning self, as the brain is functioning in an alpha state (you can read about brain waves in the next section) we are actually in a semi trance. The child brain is like a sponge absorbing information, it is like a blank tape-recording information. We thus learn our behaviour from our parents at this time, we learn what to fear and what is acceptable and unacceptable behaviour, we learn to walk by watching others doing it and copying, we learn to talk in just the same way, we are just full time mimics copying what we see around us, to give us our blue print of how to manage in the world. A child who sees a parent scream at the sight of a spider learns that a spider is to be feared, the child who sees their parent calmly pick up a spider and take it outside learns a spider is not to be feared. These are the formative years, you may have heard the expression "Give me a child from nought to seven and I will show you the man" this is why, we absorb as fact the world presented to us, which is why some people can accept extreme kinds of behaviour and others cannot, it depends on what they have been exposed to as a child. Whatever the experience, this becomes the basis for reality, as the individual knows no different. This has a huge impact on us for the rest of our lives and we spend much of them trying to unpick the learnings from our childhood. A simple example of this can be, in one household it is normal to shout at each-other, but it does not mean anything bad is happening, it is quickly forgiven and forgotten, in another household nobody shouts unless it is really serious, this means something very bad is happening. If you then put these two people in a relationship, there will be huge problems as they have different examples of normal household behaviour, one will be in a perpetual state of worry induced by the shouting and the shouter will not understand why their partner is taking this so seriously, as the patterns are in both cases subconscious, they are unlikely to understand what is happening to their relationship unless they seek help.

Coming back to this critical faculty idea, at around 5 – 7 the child begins to develop their critical faculty, this is when their sense of self really begins, their awareness of themselves as separate and they begin to challenge the views of those around them and they want to understand what it all means, they develop their conscious mind and the mind moves up into the beta state some of the time. So, they begin to ask, why? in fact they are constantly questioning what is going on around them and they begin to bring in their own interpretation of the world, it is a conscious faculty, rather than subconscious who is questioning. When we take someone into hypnosis, we bypass the critical faculty, as the conscious mind takes a back seat we have returned to the more child-like state, we the have access to the tape that was recorded so long ago and can record over it, for example removing the programming that the spider is to be feared. You can do this too in self-hypnosis, you just need a clear plan in advance of what you want to do.

Brain waves

When we become relaxed or we slip into the kind of focus we achieve in trance our brain waves change. The brain is made up of brain cells called neurons, these cells communicate with each other generating electrical pulses which are known as brain waves, we call them waves due to the flow and movement of the electrical activity, electrical pulses. These electrical communications, the pulses, can be measured via equipment which has enabled us to understand the levels of activity in the brain and interpret what is happening in the brain at different times through this measurement, we have mentioned this briefly before but let us understand it a bit more. The different brain wave states are firstly, the really alert conscious state, **Beta**. So, beta is alert consciousness, wired, active perhaps even agitated, in this state the brain is working hard to solve a problem, anything that requires focused conscious attention will generate the beta brain wave state. The electrical activity whilst in this state is measured at 13-60 pulses per second, this is measured on the Hertz scale.

The second brain wave state, the next one down that is a bit slower, less active, is **Alpha**. When the brain waves are in the alpha state, the person is relaxed both on a physical and mental level. It is often perceived to be a creative state of mind, the mind is not overly active, it can drift and be a bit dreamy, it is the state that is generated during meditation, so perhaps very familiar to some, you go into this state when in trance, you might go into it whilst playing an instrument, writing, drawing, imagining, it is accessing the lower part of the mind that storehouse of learnings, in fact, it is also deemed the ideal learning state. There is conscious awareness in this state, but there is a sense of deep calm. Endorphins like norepinephrine are released when the brain is in the Alpha state which will assist the relaxation and give a feel-good feeling. The pulses per second in this state are 7 – 13 pulses.

The third state, the next level down in brain activity is the **Theta** state. The Theta state is a somnambulistic state, it is extremely drowsy, the individual is on the very brink of slipping into sleep, there is a considerably reduced sense of conscious awareness in this state and it can be achieved when in a very deep trance, all cares and concerns will be very far away in theta, in this state 4-7 pulses per second are generated.

The final level of brain activity, right down at the bottom of the scale is **Delta**. Delta is the state of deep relaxing sleep, no conscious awareness is present at all, the brain is emitting 0.1 to 4 pulses per second. In this state healing can take place and resolution of the stress and strains of life. Attaining this state is essential to a healthy mind and body, the body chemistry recalibrates, and synaptic pruning can take place. In the brain information is stored via connections between synapses and neurons, during deep sleep certain synapses in the brain are cut, as these connect the neurons together to keep the thought, it is in simple terms a deleting process in the brain, which is vital to keep a clear mind and have space to take in new information, a bit like clearing out old files on a computer to have enough storage space. The brain marks the synapses that need to be cut with a protein marker for when the deleting process starts, in deep sleep and it makes its choice on what will get deleted by choosing to delete information that is not being used much. So, the thoughts you use a lot are the ones you will get to keep and the ones you do not, will get deleted. So if you go over and over a worry for example, the brain will decide this is information you need, it is not discerning, if there is a vital thing you want to learn like vocabulary in a new language, but you do not take the time to repeat and go over it, it will get deleted. It is useful to know just how the mind works as it will help you to make the changes that you need and want to make.

So having examined the brain wave states we can see how they relate to hypnosis, when we go into a trance state we are looking to slow the brain waves down to at least the alpha state, but many will go into theta, this is what you are aiming to do in your self-hypnosis and the you can work on those changes you want in the subconscious.

What if I fall asleep?

As we have considered that deep Delta brain wave state of sleep you might be concerned about whether you can do self-hypnosis in this brain wave state. If you find you are falling asleep whilst doing your self-hypnosis then it will be useful for you to do some recordings of the work you prepare as then if you do fall asleep, your subconscious will still be listening. Our subconscious is always listening even when our conscious mind has wandered off, when we are asleep it wakes us up if it hears an unfamiliar sound, it never stops listening. You may have had the experience of daydreaming in class at school and you thought you were not listening at all to what the teacher was saying, but if your name was said you would snap back to attention, this is because your subconscious was listening. In all my years working in hypnotherapy I have never had to shake someone awake, no matter how deeply they relax and even seem to sleep, when I ask them to open their eyes they always do. So do not worry about relaxing too deeply, but do record things for yourself if you feel you are drifting too deeply to maintain control of the experience, it does not matter if you just sleep, but for the full therapeutic benefit you need to be able to explore the ideas I will be suggesting and you cannot do that level of control in deep sleep, unless you have prepared the work and are listening to it.

Resistance

In hypnotherapy we talk a lot about resistance, someone can resist going into trance or resist the change being suggested, we look at ways to get around this resistance. With self-hypnosis you might think that resistance would not be an issue as you have decided to do the work on yourself, but this is also the case if you consult a therapist, you are paying them to help you, so why would you resist that help? I come back to the idea of the conscious and subconscious mind again, you might consciously decide to, for example to stop smoking, this decision is made consciously, but that subconscious part of your mind that has learned the smoking habit will sometimes put up a show of resistance to that change, after all it is only doing what you taught it to do, so it will keep trying to do it.

As we have discussed we learn many habits, patterns and behaviours, many of which are good for us, your subconscious is not discerning in this, it just follows its continued pattern. So even in self-hypnosis we are looking at different ways to bypass this resistance, ways around it, such as hiding the idea within a story or metaphor, using indirect instructions tor using the power of repetition to get around that block. Even though you are putting the ideas there, you know you are trying to trick the subconscious with these ideas, they will still work for you, in the same way as they would work if someone else were making these suggestions to you. We will look at all these ideas in the "what to do in trance" section.

The Power of Suggestion

What is Suggestion?

The power of suggestion is key to the success of the self-hypnosis process and indeed healing of all kinds, as if you do not believe you will recover, your recovery will be slower and perhaps even limited. The importance of the power of suggestion has been a part of healing for many centuries but was acknowledged for its importance with the work of a French pharmacist called Emile Coué in the late 19th Century. Like many advances in medicine his discovery came about by accident. One day a patient who was always complaining about something, one of those people who always had a problem came into Coué's pharmacy, his heart sank as he had given him everything he could think of to help him and was running out of ideas, he was also very busy on this particular day, so to get rid of him quickly he gave him a plain solution of water and a small amount of sugar, but told him it was a new treatment that had just arrived from Paris and was affecting wonderful cures. The patient returned a couple of days later hailing the cure as a miracle, he was completely better, the wonder medicine from Paris had completely cured him. Coué thought about this for some time and realised that it was simply the belief that the medicine was going to work, that had cured him, so he thought it must be possible to harness this belief to create all sorts of change and he launched a form of healing that became known as Couéism, which utilised the power of suggestion to affect change. This became very popular in the USA in the 1920s. We can see a strong link here to the placebo effect which most people would now acknowledge has credibility and we will be examining this further.

People can achieve incredible feats of strength when they harness their belief in themselves and people have been known to show resistance to infection through the power of belief, perhaps belief that their God protects them, or they are in some way special. There is a case of a religious sect in America where people are encouraged to expose themselves to being bitten by deadly poisonous snakes to prove that God will protect them and their belief is so strong that they do not die, this same belief can be seen in much faith healing, though of course you can argue that God is doing the healing if you have a strong faith. Though faith, belief, the power of suggestion has power for those with no religious beliefs too, it depends on the source of your faith in the process.

We can look at this power in very simple terms too, you may have experienced feeling uplifted and more energised when someone says to you "you look great today" conversely if someone says "you look tired, did you have a bad night?" we can find ourselves aware of a feeling of malaise not there before and your shoulders sag with hitherto undetected tiredness.

The Placebo

The therapeutic benefits of suggestion are most widely acknowledged through the use of the placebo, simply thousands of pieces of research exist to prove the impact of belief in medical treatments. Cancer patients with inoperable tumours have gone into remission after being given placebos, wrapped up as new wonder drugs; they have even done placebo operations with knee surgery, telling a patient that work has been done to repair a damaged knee, when nothing could be done to help and the patient becomes able to walk normally again. Let's look at some evidence, JAMA published a research paper in 1989 "Randomised double bind trial of intravenous Prochlorperazine for treatment of acute headache" (J Jones, D Sclar, J Doughety) in this trial some people were given the migraine drug and some a placebo, 45% of the people in the placebo group reported partial or complete relief from their headache pain. Another major study used sham acupuncture for IBS sufferers, from Neurogastroenterol Motif 2017 (C Lowe, Aitken T, Day AG, Vanner SJ) Sham acupuncture is as effective as acupuncture for the treatment of IBS. In this trial 42% of people reported relief from the sham acupuncture. I am sure you have already heard of many other trials so I will not pursue this any further here, only to say that from all the research out there, the efficacy of the placebo seems to be more and more accepted, even stated as pertinent to the impact on allopathic (traditional) medicine in the Government White Paper into the efficacy of complementary medicine in 2000.

The Nocebo

The word "nocebo" means, to cause harm in Latin and has been adopted into the language as the opposite to the placebo. We have to understand that the power of suggestion can work both ways and the negative impact of suggestion can be just as powerful as the positive, so the things people say and do may affect us in a negative way, even what we say to ourselves can affect us. We just have to think about the concept of the witch doctor who tells a perfectly healthy person they are going to die and die they do, simply because they believe they will. A great deal of research is going into this area at the moment, Ernil Hanson, a German Doctor is one of the leading lights in this research, in an article in the journal Pharmacol in 2019, he highlights his concerns that that language doctors use with patients can affect how they recover and even the level of pain they might feel.

To take this our understanding further I would like to cite an anti-depressant clinical drug trial in 2007, published in General Hospital Psychiatry (Reeves RR, Ladnor ME, Hart RH, Burke RS) this details the case of a patient in a drug trial for anti-depressants taking an overdose with the intention of killing himself, but the tablets were a placebo with no chemical elements, he became very ill as he believed he had taken an overdose and was rushed to hospital, he only began to show signs of recovery when he was told that the tablets were not anti-depressants, the simple belief that the pills were deadly made him dangerously ill. Why is this important to us? In everyday life we receive negative signals which can be affecting us, this also proves conclusively the power of the mind over the body.

This also raises the issue of the mind/body connection. The way we think effects our body beyond the stress fight or flight issues which we will look at later. I have often thought the famous Descartes quote "I think therefore I am" could be interpreted to mean how I think impacts on how I am, as our thought processes have such a clear impact on our physical health.

If we accept this evidence of both placebo and nocebo and we have just scratched the surface here, then it becomes important to consider the language medics use when talking to patients, as they will respond to suggestions of increased pain for example and we need to consider the language we use with each other and the language we use with ourselves, our internal dialogue, to limit negative impact and enhance the positive ones.

We can harness this belief to heal ourselves using direct and indirect suggestion, metaphor and skilful use of language. None of us like to think we are suggestible, but actually most of us are and it is not a bad thing if we start using it for our highest benefit.

Testing your response to suggestion

A useful way to examine your own suggestibility is to follow this simple visualisation. I would like you to imagine that you are holding a lemon in your hand, feel the bumpy surface of the lemon, perhaps noticing the waxy texture of the lemon, notice the bright yellow colour of the lemon, notice the shape of the lemon, now place this lemon onto a surface which you will be able to cut the lemon into two pieces, pick up a knife and slice the lemon in two, you may even hear the sound of the knife as it cuts the lemon and maybe touches the cutting surface, put the knife down and pick up one of the lemon halves, now bring it up to your nose, sniff it, I wonder if you can get the zesty smell of the lemon, there may be a little of the lemon juice running onto your finger-tips. Now run your tongue over the centre of the lemon pulp, getting that sharp taste upon your tongue as the juice trickles over it, you may find yourself swallowing as you respond to the juice, your mouth may even water at the thought of tasting that lemon juice, now put the lemon down again and bring yourself back to full attention to the world around you. Now that you know this exercise, rather than reading it through, close your eyes and repeat the exercise again and see if it makes the experience and the response of your senses more powerful. How your senses respond, how clear your find the images, whether you swallow or salivate will all indicate to some extent your response to suggestion.

Some people are far more suggestable than others, in some cases you just have to mention feeling like yawning and someone listening to you will yawn, or perhaps the mention of the word swallowing will trigger the automatic impulse to swallow. These are of course very obvious as they involve a physical response, but many of the suggestions we are responding to daily involve a psychological response. For example, if you tell someone they are useless and stupid regularly they will develop low self-esteem and struggle to achieve anything.

Now we can do a follow up test to assess further and in more depth your response to suggestion, do not be put off if you find you are answering yes to some of these questions, it means you are a great subject for self-hypnosis.

Suggestibility Test

Questions require yes/no answers   Score for yes answer

1. Do you read a lot of fiction? **1 point**
2. Do you laugh easily? **1 point**
3. If I describe the sound of rustling leaves upon a tree or the sound of the crackle of a fire in the grate, the sound of the sea on the beach, can you hear any of these sounds? **2 points**
4. If I describe the smell of wet damp earth, the smell of burning rubber, the smell of a freshly cut lawn, the smell on an open fire, can you create in your mind any of these smells? **2 points**
5. Do you fall in and out of love easily/rapidly? **1 point**
6. If I ask you to visualise the blue of the sea and the rolling white foam spray rolling up the beach as it rolls in and out, or to visualise your front door to your home, or maybe see in your mind's eye the last place you went on holiday, can you see any of these images in your mind? **2 points**
7. If I say I feel tired and want to yawn, I can feel a huge yawn coming, stretching my jaws wide with the yawn, do you feel any impulse at all to yawn, any reaction at all to this statement? **2 points**
8. If I describe the sharp bitter tang of a lemon juice in your mouth, bitter and sharp, does your mouth water? **2 points**
9. If I describe the feeling of the sun warming your skin, a warm fire warming your skin or perhaps suggest that you have an itch somewhere, a tickly itchy sensation somewhere on your skin, do you feel any of those sensations? **2 points**
10. Do you get addicted to dramatic TV sagas like Game of Thrones? **1 point**

SUGGESTIBILITY TEST

11. Do you avoid certain types of films or books as they will cause nightmares or make you too distressed? **2 points**

12. Do you rerun conversations in your head after social gatherings, perhaps thinking of other things you might have said? **2 points**

13. Would you describe yourself as someone who likes an audience, someone who likes to entertain? **2 points**

14. Do you feel uncomfortable if someone you do not know well stands close to you whilst talking to you? **1 point**

15. Have you ever found yourself copying the way someone is sitting, or perhaps their hand gestures or other body movements? **2 points**

16. Have you ever found yourself using a word that you had not used before because you have heard someone else use it, or repeating a sentence or phrase that someone else has just said back to them in agreement, using their words? **2 points**

17. Do you believe in things that you cannot see with your eyes or hear with your ears? **1 point**

18. Would you describe yourself as emotional? **1 point**

19. If someone offers you another drink, or something more to eat, do you take it when you do not want it if they ask you one or more times? **2 points**

20. Do you cry easily? **1 point**

21. Would you describe yourself as a worrier? **2 points**

22. Have you ever bought something on the strength of an advertisement? **1 point**

23. Would you describe yourself as a day dreamer? **1 point**

24. Do you do any creative writing? **1 point**

25. Do you paint pictures? **1 point**

Scoring

- 0-5   Low level of suggestibility
- 6-10.   Limited suggestibility
- 11-29.   Very suggestible
- 30+.   Highly suggestible.

The Mind Body Relationship

We have already begun to consider the mind body relationship through looking at the power of suggestion, the placebo and the nocebo are both clear indicators that what is going on in the mind can affect the body. Now we are going to look at the effect of stress on the body which causes so many of the problems both physical and mental that people are facing today. The stress response is completely automatic and not consciously controlled, but our response to stressful situations can exacerbate how often that response is triggered. Any form of self-help must address this automatic response of the autonomic nervous system and work on calming this system down into an appropriate response system, not reacting to perceived threats everywhere. Once we have found ways to impact on our stress response many other factors in our lives will become much easier.

The Stress Response

The stress response was designed to get us out of real danger, physical danger, originally to escape from predators like a sabre tooth tiger and we still need it today, for example, to get us away from a car coming onto the pavement or escape from a mugger. However, most of the time that stress response is working on perceived threats rather than real practical danger. Fears of losing a job, one's home, a relationship, pressure from a boss at work, even pressures created by perceived visibility in social media and wanting to be a success in everything, will trigger our stress response into action. The pressures out there seem to be growing with each decade, when young people are committing suicide from cyber bullying, we must acknowledge our society is creating huge strain in our lives. These kinds of perceived threats will not be assisted by the stress response, if anything it hampers our ability to deal with these threats as the mind no longer thinks clearly, these kind of threats need a cerebral rather than a physical solution.

When the subconscious mind picks up on a perceived threat it swings into action to help us to escape the situation, to fight to protect ourselves, to run away or even to freeze so that our enemy cannot see us, in that basic primal way of hiding in the long grass. Blood flow is diverted from the digestive system towards the limbs to assist with escape from danger; this leaves the digestive system under-supported leading to problems like indigestion and nausea. The immune system is also left unsupported so there is an increased risk of infections.

To assist the ability to run, the body can have diarrhoea, literally getting rid of excess baggage, this can also apply to the bladder and lead to continence issues. Blood flow is diverted away from the thinking frontal part of the brain to the hind brain, which leads to an impairment of the decision-making process, we literally cannot think clearly, and we become governed by the basic hind brain. Our heart rate increases to facilitate getting the blood supply where it is needed, people can sometimes feel like they are having a heart attack as the heart is racing so fast. There is an increased breath rate, to get oxygen to where it is needed for optimum physical performance, this can lead to hyperventilation, whereby there is an imbalance of oxygen and carbon dioxide in the blood, usually too little carbon dioxide which alters blood flow and affecting the nerve response, this leads to weakness and sometimes numbness and pins and needles. People who suffer from panic attacks will often experience hyperventilation and it is a really scary feeling, combined with the increased heart rate, people often feel like they are about to die, and this makes the whole situation worse.

There is chemical activity going on as well when the stress response kicks in; cholesterol is pumped into the bloodstream to provide a boost of energy for flight, but this leaves fatty deposits behind and can lead to heart disease and stroke; cortisol is released from the adrenal glands giving protection from allergy during a short crisis period, but long-term release of cortisol weakens the immune system; adrenalin is released to produce a burst of speed, but long-term exposure to adrenalin causes jumpy agitated behaviour, it is adrenalin that causes sweating in a panic attack and of course that accelerated heart rate.

This is merely a snapshot of what is actually happening in your body when you get stressed, most of us know some of this, maybe not all of this, but we rely on our body to sort it out and pay it little attention. In modern society it seems a given that people accept being in this state a lot of the time, but our body was not designed to be in this state for long periods of time and it is creating a huge impact on our health.

People usually only address the situation and feel they need to do something about it when it escalates to a full panic attack, or sleeplessness from all the adrenalin makes them feel ill. When looking at self-help and thinking of using self-hypnosis to achieve this, as well as any other reason you may have picked up this book, do not ignore your stress response anymore, even some simple relaxation techniques will help you begin to take back control and reprogram that response. We need to reserve that stress response for situations of real and practical danger not emotional and psychological pressures, because it cannot help us with these in fact, as I have said, it will almost certainly make the situation worse.

How to get into a trance

There are various ways to access the trance state most involving visualisation processes, or the kind of body scan that may be familiar to you if you have ever experienced meditation. We can also access a state of auto suggestion via a series of cue words. There is a fine line between deep meditation and trance, both involve accessing the alpha brain wave state and it is hard to say where one ends and the other begins, the key to the success though is what you do when you access this state, that state of focused attention, often including some degree of relaxation.

With the visualisation processes, I suggest that you read through the ideas and then re-create them quietly and slowly in your mind, or you can even record them onto a phone or Dictaphone and listen to them. In these, I give clear directions, but in the therapeutic work you will be addressing yourself. The visual based exercises are best for people who see images easily in their minds, think about which of your senses you recreate most easily in your mind, you may find sounds are more clear for you or even sensations, focus on what helps you to engage in the experience most, it could be one or maybe all of your senses, for some it is just accessing an idea or a concept.

Cue words

Choose a word that you would like to be your trigger word for going into trance, it is sometimes an idea to use a more obscure word, one you will not be using regularly, or perhaps a word that links to how you want to feel, like drowsy, or maybe something which you can visualise easily like a colour perhaps, you can try different ideas until you find what works best for you. I always use the colour "Blue" as my word.

You will be using the word that you have chosen to get you into trance three times in the following way: State the word that you have chosen once you have found a comfortable place for your self-hypnosis session and close your eyes to shut out any external distractions. Now give all your attention to your head, aware of the muscles in your face that do so much work for you, communicating your feelings through your expression, allow the muscles to loosen as you give them attention and move away from your head down into your neck, your head is often packed full of chasing thoughts so we want to move down into the body, you may have done a body scan in meditation before and that is similar to what we are doing now, taking your attention down through your shoulders, your arms into your hands, into your fingers and thumbs, just noticing as you go, just giving each part of your body that you visit your full attention for a moment, not for long, it does not need to feel like a torturous slow exercise, but just flowing through your body, down your back into your pelvis and noticing, moving down your chest into your abdomen, moving through to the tops of your legs and then following this flow of attention, loosening those muscles as you go, down your legs into your feet, noticing any sensations there, any feeling on the soles of the feet, the feeling in your toes and when you have completed this journey through your body, now tell yourself you have reached a place of stillness ready to do the work.

Now say your cue word for a second time.

You are ready now to focus on the work today, some simple direct suggestions and affirmations work well with this technique rather than some of the more complex metaphor ideas we will examine, so working through what you want to do.

Then when you are ready to finish today, repeat the word a third time and you will become fully alert again and as you have programmed your mind in this way, it will expect to return to full consciousness when you state the word a third time.

Eye Closure

One of the most common ways to obtain the trance state is called eye closure, it requires you to imagine that your eyelids are really heavy, so imagine that now, imagine your eyelids are so very heavy and sleepy, you may start by staring at something upon the wall, a fixed point, one of little interest that will not arouse a commentary in your head, maybe the top of a picture frame or a light fitting, keep your eyes staring at this until they start to feel heavy, perhaps you can imagine when you are reading a book and your eyes get heavier and heavier, your eyes will be feeling heavier and heavier and they just want to close, it is a struggle to keep them open, they get heavier and heavier with each breath you take and then finally, finally they snap shut. Now you will have read this before so you know that when they snap shut, so heavy and tired, they just do not want to work anymore, you can say this to yourself that they do not want to work anymore they are so comfortable closed that if you were to try to open them they would just stay shut, shutting out the light, shutting out the day and you do not have to force them to stay open any more, what a relief, you may even find yourself releasing a deep sigh as you realise that you can keep your eyes closed, peacefully closed and get on with the work you want to do in your mind today. Sometimes if we lead very busy lives, just the very suggestion that the eyelids are feeling heavy will create the desired result, as it is something that we all associate with tiredness and with relaxing.

Wipers

Just imagine that you are in a car, a simple visualisation just for now, you are in the car and it is raining, but you are not driving this car, you are being driven, so you can relax back in the passenger seat and go along for the ride, the rain is hitting the windscreen, so the windscreen wipers are on, imagining this now and making the image even clearer, seeing the windscreen wipers moving from side to side, sweeping back and forth, back and forth, you may find yourself watching those wipers as they move back and forth, back and forth and you can easily create this image in your mind, when you want to slip into trance to do some work for you, watching that steady movement back and forth, you might even find yourself moving and swaying with that rhythm, but noticing even more detail now, in this rainy scene, driving along in the car, the rain is hitting the windscreen and you can see the splats of water hitting the screen and drizzling down, running down the glass and then the wipers come along and sweep it away and then it starts again, more rain again, hitting the windscreen and beginning its journey down the glass and now hearing that rain as it hits the glass, that pattering sound of the rain smattering, pattering against the glass as you drift deeper into trance and the wipers may make a sound too, most wipers do, that swiping, wiping sound moving across the glass, swish, swish, the sounds anchoring you there in the image and the clear goblets of water hitting the screen and you seeing it there and then there is the back and forth, back and forth as the wipers keep the windscreen clear, so you can see the road up ahead, but what matters right now is seeing this scene in your mind and allowing trance to occur, only when you see this in your mind, this journey in your mind, taking you into trance, drifting into that quiet space where you can do the work you want to do for you, that's right.

Numbers

Using numbers and forms of counting to relax the mind is very common, using a very visual process to do this will make it much easier, a way to distract the mind. Once you have settled yourself into a comfortable position, a quiet place where you will not be disturbed, once you have read this through, close your eyes and begin to allow your mind to focus in on your body for a moment, and then come into your mind and imagine, see in your mind's-eye you are picking up a small note book/note pad, when you open it you see the number 100 on the page in front of you, nothing else, just 100, I want you to tear out that page and you will see revealed beneath it is another page and it has 99 written on it, I would like you to tear that page out now revealing the number 98 below, now we are going to tear that page out too now and 97 is there, as you concentrate on the numbers and tearing each page out once the number is revealed, looking at the numbers each time one is revealed to you, you find yourself feeling surprisingly relaxed, perhaps hearing the sound of the page as it tears, aware of the texture of the paper in your hand, watching the numbers go down and down, one page after another revealing the number below, it is like opening Russian dolls and seeing the dolls get smaller and smaller, the numbers are getting smaller and smaller, as the numbers get smaller and smaller you relax deeper and deeper, I wonder if you can notice how deeply you relax, as the numbers get smaller and smaller, as the number of torn pages grows, piled up beside you there, the written numbers get smaller and you go deeper and deeper. Page after page, the numbers descending like going down in a lift, down and down, focusing all of your attention on the numbers as they go down and down and taking you into trance, allowing yourself to drift right down into trance, that's right so you can do the work you want to do today, when the pad is empty the numbers all gone you will be in a comfortable trance, or it may be you realise that you do not need all of those numbers to get you into trance, it is up to you as you are in control of this process of relaxing your mind, maybe all the numbers are gone now until you need them again, they will always be there for you to take you down, each time you practice this it will get easier and easier to go deeper and deeper into trance now.

Hot air balloon

I would like you to imagine that you are standing on a beach and there is a blue sky above you and you are looking up there into the blue, blue sky, it is bright up there because the sun is shining, but you think that you can see something up there in the sky, something is descending down gracefully and slowly from above, your eyes may feel a bit tired from looking up there now, very tired there now, as you strain looking up into the sky and you realise that it is a bright hot air balloon that you can see, see the colours of the balloon and the basket hanging beneath the balloon, it is still so high in the sky, but you can see it now, use all your ability to concentrate to focus on the balloon as it gradually moves nearer and nearer to the ground and your eyes are tired now and you are relaxing more and more as you watch the balloon swaying its way down towards to ground, keep looking up though, concentrating on that balloon, noticing the colours there, aware of the bright light in the sky, you may be aware of a gust of air, the air that gently sways the balloon like the rocking of a baby in the cot, rocking, the basket beneath the balloon, rocking from side to side, swaying and rocking, some way away from you, watching it closely and carefully and relaxing more and more and before that graceful colourful balloon has touched the ground, you will have found that you are in a deep trance, the balloon has taken you down as it moves towards the ground taking you into trance now so that you can do the work that you need to do now.

Body scan

One of the simplest and most traditional ways of relaxing and inducing trance is doing a scan of the body as is often done in mindful meditation, we touched on this with the cue words, but this would be a more detailed, slower progress through the body. It takes the mind away from the focus on active thought, but rather sensation, also all the cues are there and easy to follow, just following either up or down the body, most people start from the head as then you are flowing down with your focus.

So to begin, focus all your attention on the very top of your head, just holding all of your attention there and then moving into your face, making sure your eyes are closed to shut out distractions aware of how comfortable it is to close your eyes whatever the time of day is and focus on all the small muscles in your face, they do so much work each day, as they express your feelings and thoughts, so allowing those muscles to loosen and lengthen and giving the jaw permission to unclench, notice how just taking your attention to your jaw makes it loosen, perhaps only slightly and allowing the tongue to lie loosely in the mouth, you may find yourself swallowing for a moment because your attention is in your mouth and then we can move into the neck, you might want to move it from side to side for a moment to allow the tension to drain out of your neck, make sure your back is supported so that you can now allow that focus and relaxation to move into your shoulders, from there we just slowly take the focus down the arms, upper and lower, into the hands and fingers, allowing the muscles to loosen and relax as you go, you might want to give your attention to the right arm first and then the left, or perhaps the left and then the right, as you do so noticing if one side of your body is relaxing more quickly than the other, as you give attention to your finger-tips, then back to the back, upper and lower, just noticing anything you might feel there as you go and not rushing the process taking your time, you might even imagine going down each vertebrate one at a time bouncing over the nobbles there, then down your front, over your chest and into the abdomen, allowing yourself to become more aware of your breaths as your chest rises and falls, noticing the gentle flow of the air in and out of your body, that vital energy source, maybe holding the attention on those breaths a moment or two more, notice the cool air as it touches your top lip and enters your nose and the warmer air as it flows out again, really noticing the powerful rise and fall of the chest and that expansion in the chest, the powerful rise of the abdomen, notice this before you move down past your hips and genital region and into your legs and as with the arms you may decide on the right side first or maybe the left, but following down the thighs into the lower leg, giving awareness to the shins, ankles and into the feet, perhaps noticing any sensations in the soles of the feet, across the bridge of the foot and taking the attention across each toe in turn, I wonder if one foot is more relaxed than the other right now, you can consider this and I wonder if you will have noticed that your mind has calmed and if you are not yet completely relaxed taking your attention back to the breath as you prepare to do the work you need to do in your subconscious mind today.

Self-hypnosis outdoors

Some people find they can go into trance more easily in an outdoors setting, somewhere in nature. There is a growing movement for both self-hypnosis and hypnotherapy in the outdoors, Eco-hynotherapy.

To experience this for yourself, find a place in an outdoor setting where you can be comfortable and will not be disturbed, perhaps lying on the sand, or on a rug in a meadow or in the woods. Now firstly look around you, use your eyes to take in detail that would normally be over looked, really see the shapes around you, see the colours of nature around you, trying to switch off your other senses and channel everything into your sight, see clearly, watch for any movement in your landscape, now when you are ready to go deeper, close your eyes, now recreate that scene in your mind, see it clearly as you just did, as clear as you can then move away from the visual sense for a moment and for a while sound will become more prominent, really focus on what you can hear, sounds of birds perhaps, the sound of a gentle breeze, just listen, you may even hear your breath, your breaths in and out, what can you hear now? Focus in and listen, listen with all of your attention, hear sounds you take for granted as background, bring them into the foreground, that's right, now I would like you to take yourself into your sense of touch, this may seem hard at first but what sensations can you feel on your skin, can you feel the sun on your skin, or is it the coolness of the air, can you feel the air cool on your top lip before you breathe it in and then warm as you breathe it out, are there shoes on your feet, can you feel them if they are there, material against your skin, allow this sense to be centre stage giving it all of your attention and now you have focused your senses, and what about smell, can you smell anything here, a natural smell that anchors you in this place, what can you smell, really stretch that sense to its limit, really pull any smell into your nose, be aware of it and process it, now you have given yourself this focus on this beautiful place and really moved away from that racing chasing mind, you are ready to go deep within your mind and do the work you need to do today.

Coming out of trance

Will I wake up?

One of the main issues that needs to be addressed when you are dealing with self-hypnosis is the fear many have of not being able to wake themselves up. Some people have this fear generally in hypnosis and the fear can be allayed in a similar way. If you were to fall asleep in front of the television or drift off to sleep in the train or being driven in the car, you do not worry that you will not wake up. In self-hypnosis we will be using certain ways to stimulate the waking from trance, but you would no more get stuck in a trance state, any more than you would not wake up from an afternoon nap or doze in front of the television. So, you are quite safe and sometimes allowing your mind a bit of extra time to come out of trance when it wants to, is not a bad thing, it means that there was some extra work to do. In my work as a therapist, I have never experienced a person not coming out of trance when I asked them to.

How to come out of trance

Cues

The person using self-hypnosis can use cue words that the subconscious will recognise as the cue to wake up, but if for any reason the person where to miss the cue it would be no different to waking naturally from sleep. You can work out these cues when you are in a fully conscious state.

Counting out

Another option to give for coming out of trance is to use the same numerical counting out process, when you feel you want to stop the process you have been working on just counting up from 1-3 or 1-5 whatever feels more comfortable for you, but decide in advance if this is going to be your awakening/coming out of trance procedure. It is of course very simple if you are recording something to listen to, simply say "I am going to count from one to three and by the time I reach the count of three you will be fully alert again" or you might want to use the first person when in your mind, "I will be fully alert again"

Time limit

Setting a time limit for the trance can also give a sense of security, as the minds inner clock will also be working as well as the link into the numbers or cue word. You could set an alarm to go off, a simple bell to chime to mark the end of the session if this increases your level of security. Many people use this to mark their period of meditation and it is just as helpful in self-hypnosis.

Coming out of trance naturally

You can of course decide to come out of trance naturally when the moment feels right for your conscious mind to fully return. When you go to sleep at night or have an afternoon nap your subconscious will ultimately wake you up, we do not lie down to sleep and like sleeping beauty stay there forever more, when we are suitably rested or if an unexpected sound is heard we wake up, so there is no chance of being lost in a trance state forever more. You have a good understanding of trance now, so it should be clear that the trance state is a natural one, that there are just the options of awake, asleep and a drowsy in-between state, the state of focused attention which gives that zoned out feeling. We are not looking in self-hypnosis to achieve a state of totally unconscious and if that were to happen, you have just fallen asleep.

In self-hypnosis as you need to be in charge of giving positive suggestions to your subconscious, you will not be going as deeply as you might with a hypnotherapist, unless you decide to make recordings of the work that you do.

What to do in trance

We can use a range of different ideas when we have achieved the trance state, this is the actual therapy part, that you can use to help make changes for yourself, we will look at how these ideas work and then you will be given a variety of examples that you can work with, broken down into different areas of therapy, also giving some further explanation within each section. You do not have to make your session complicated, you can keep to simple affirmations and direct suggestions, or you may want to develop into doing something more complex and experiment with indirect suggestions and metaphors. Some of the language patterns may seem a bit strange at first and in some cases the language may seem repetitive, but that is the style of hypnotic language.

Direct Suggestions

Direct suggestion within hypnosis is the use of a direct command to create a change in behaviour. Sometimes it is just a case of focusing in on the area of desired change and giving it the instruction that it wants and needs to hear.

It works well in various areas such as insomnia, phobia and addictions. The command should always be in the present tense, not the future tense, so that it is a foregone conclusion that the change has been affected, you have achieved it, it is done. It is a reality in the present not something that is yet to happen.

Now we are going to look at some examples of direct suggestions across a range of treatment areas, these are not affirmations which are often much shorter:

"I will feel no need, craving or desire to smoke tobacco in any form again. If I am in the company of other smokers and someone offers me a cigarette, I will say I do not smoke, that will feel natural for me to say. Wherever I am, at home alone or out with friends, I will feel no need, craving or desire for tobacco of any kind."

"When I go to bed at night, I am going to bed to sleep, I will go to bed, to go into a deep refreshing sleep, nothing will stop me now from attaining a deep, long refreshing sleep."

"From the moment I wake up today, I will only want to eat at mealtimes, I will only want to eat at mealtimes, never tempted to eat at any other time, I will eat in small amounts the food I need to be well and strong, I can control my weight, I can achieve the weight I want to be" With regard to weight control, it is important to think about the language. If we say weight loss, it can result in resisting because you do not want to lose something, loss is never a good word to use so, try to avoid it, we are working with weight control.

Indirect Suggestion

Our minds do not always like being told what to do, even when we are doing the telling! So that is why we also use what we call indirect suggestions, we can use them often in combination with direct suggestions as a way of combating resistance to the direct commands. It is the subtlety of an indirect suggestion that can bypass our resistance, our barriers to change, I guess what we are doing is tricking the subconscious mind into doing what we want it to do. We will look at some examples to help you to understand how to use them.

You can follow a direct suggestion with something like ... "and this is not something that I will not find easy." When you unravel this sentence, it is actually saying it will be easy as the two negative cancel each other out, but if you just said it would be easy, the mind might block the suggestion, in saying it this way it confuses the deep part of the mind into submission and accepting that it will be easy.

A similar approach is used in "The person who cannot achieve this is not the person that is feeling so relaxed right now." In this you are using the same two negatives, but also speaking in the third person, again tricking your mind into accepting that you can do the thing that you are trying to do, your mind will just accept it. Some of these indirect suggestions might be easier used on a recording, rather than working just within your mind, as they are a bit complicated, but you could write them down as part of a recording you are doing for yourself.

Some other examples involve using a law of the mind called the Law of Reverse effect, when we use this, the harder we try to do something the more difficult it becomes, you may have heard of the old mind challenge "try not to think about a pink elephant", when you do this of course all you can think about is a pink elephant, so we use this within therapy as in:

"I do not want to notice too often how much more confident I am feeling" So if you are really trying not to notice how much more confident you are feeling, as when trying not to think of the pink elephant, all you will notice is how much more confident you are feeling. We can use this idea for addictions really well, for example: "I am going to try not to notice how easy it is to walk past a betting shop" If you try not to notice it at all, you will notice how easy it is to walk past the betting shop.

These suggestions encourage the brain to process a positive concept before it negates it. For example if I say "don't trip" your mind has to process what it means to trip before it turns it into a negative, so in many respects this is not a helpful suggestion, it is more likely to lead to tripping, it is better for the mind to be told a positive like be careful, however it is a useful process for what we want to achieve. In many respects we are using confusion with some of these suggestions, because of its very nature causes the mind to give in and accept what it is being told because it is confused, it is easier than trying to unravel the meaning of what is being said.

This may seem rather complicated, but you do not have to fully understand why it works, just accept it does work and try it out, following the examples in the appropriate section of the book. The indirect suggestion is the way of making a command via a circuitous route. It is useful to weave indirect suggestion into every session if you can.

A softer indirect approach can be:

"I wonder if I can notice...how calm and relaxed I am feeling" this will meet less resistance than "I am feeling calm."

This suggestion cleverly utilises what we call presupposition, by saying "I wonder if I can notice how calm I am feeling" you are immediately presupposing that you do feel calm, it is just a matter of whether you will notice it or not! Your mind will then stop resisting the idea of the concept of calm, it is so much easier for the mind than simply saying, "I am calm" as this is more likely to be greeted by resistance from your mind, the indirect approach sneaks under your radar and leads to an acceptance of reaching a calm mind state. Try it out when you can, perhaps when you are feeling more confident with the process.

Metaphors

A metaphor is simply a story with a hidden meaning, a meaning that our subconscious mind will understand, it strengthens the message through the use of the imagery, ideas and associations. If we say: "I can see the light at the end of the tunnel" the imagery makes the message so much stronger than just saying things are going to get better, so we utilise this within self-hypnosis and in hypnotherapy to help the mind to process useful ideas. The metaphor provides us with the connection, the link, the route for that change. We are all programmed to respond to metaphor, we use metaphors every day to emphasise a message, to enforce meaning, to clarify meaning. Every culture has its own metaphors and some move across cultures, part of the universal unconscious perhaps.

Metaphor is powerful because of its subtlety, its familiarity and its associations with the security of childhood. We are told stories by our parents when we are children, it is associated with relaxing, being comfortable and safe. We learn from stories at an early age through parable, fables and fairy tales, we are conditioned to understand and look for the messages within. It gives meaning with subtlety.

When you are using these, if you are not recording it to listen to, but are going to work within your mind, read the script a few times to get the essence of it and focus on the ideas in it, you do not need to remember all the language. Let us look at a metaphor we might use in self-hypnosis just to make it clear.

This is a metaphor I use for someone who is pining over a lost relationship that they thought was right for them, but had not worked out, it is called "The Right Fit" and comes from my book "The Healing Metaphor"

I wonder if you have had this experience....an experience that I have had before.......you walk past a shop window....there is something in there that you would love to wear....a dress...or a jacket....summer....or winter....maybe a new autumn fashion.... you really love it...you see yourself in it....imagine yourself ....imagine yourself looking wonderful in it....you may pass the shop from time to time....perhaps on the way to work.....each time you look longingly at the outfit...thinking how well it would suit you....it is expensive so you have to think about it....it hovers in your mind...how good you would look in it.....you decide you must have it.....you have just enough money....so pleased at last to be getting the outfit...you go into the shop....you decide you had better try it on...with certainty you pick your size from the rail...go into the changing room ....you try it on.....when you look in the mirror...it is not a bit how you saw it....the fit just is not right for you....you cannot believe it....you were so sure that this was the one.....the one for you....but it just does not fit right....the fit is all wrong....at first you are so disappointed....you had set your heart on it...thought about it for so long...you were just so sure that this was the look for you...an assistant sees you sadly putting it back on the rail and you explain your disappointment to them...they smile and point out all the other clothes on the rail...there is so much else there....why did it have to be this particular one...but you had set your heart on it...this was the outfit for you...but after some persuasion you pick another couple of outfits from the rail...go back into the changing rooms...then try one on and look in the mirror...you look fantastic...this look is so right for you...the cut is so flattering...you feel so good as you look in the mirror...this is the one for you....you cannot understand why you had got so fixed on that other one...it was just not right for you...so you go outside and buy this new outfit...so pleased to have found the right thing for you...you just needed to open your mind to the other choices and look at what else that was there...not stay fixed on that one in the window... that one would suit someone else but was just not for you....your subconscious mind understands the stories that I tell...the meaning of my words...and can make all the changes that you need to make now...the changes to open your mind... open your mind to new possibilities...to leave the past behind... that's right....as you continue to relax....

So, this in an indirect way, gets your mind to consider that the relationship had not really been perfect, you were trying to make it seem so and that something better is around the corner, but if we say this in direct terms, our mind will try to resist it. This particular metaphor also uses something called "truisms", truisms are things that most of us have probably experienced already and really resonated with us, you get that, "oh yes, I know what you mean" feeling. I guess the metaphor is just another way of tricking the mind into changing and you will see many of these metaphors within this book.

When choosing metaphors to work with, there are ideas within this book that may not be listed in the section relating to your problem but may be useful, such as the script called "The Mind a screen", the positive resource state or self-appreciation, which can be applied to many situations, so read through the ideas in the book to see what might apply to your situation.

Affirmations

Affirmations are simple statements repeated like a mantra, doing this at least ten times within a trance state can impact on the intention within the subconscious mind. Repetition is an important way to re-enforce any belief as it is how we learn. After all that is how we learned that two plus two equals four, we say it enough times and we know it. We are enforcing connections in the neural pathways in the mind when we repeat things, hear it enough and it becomes your truth. This is great when we are doing positive affirmations but they can be negative, for example, if someone is repeatedly telling you something unkind like "You are useless", this has an impact on us, we respond to that negative suggestion and feel useless. We can say negative things to ourselves too, if we repeatedly say negative things to ourselves we can believe them to be true, in fact, much of what we are doing within therapy is to undo constant negative input, sometimes external but often internal, we begin to believe the "I am useless statements" if said often enough, but it can therefore work the other way around if we put our effort into it and emphasise the positives. We need to counteract any negative statements with the opposite. Always state the affirmation in the present tense as if it is something that is already achieved, not in the future yet to be achieved. For example: "I am free of fear, fear is not a part of my life now".

Future Pacing

Future pacing is a very simple visualisation exercise which can be very powerful when done in trance. When you have done some work in trance using some metaphors or suggestions, you then visualise yourself as you want to be, as clearly as you can and then bring the good feelings you can feel from having achieved this

WHAT TO DO IN TRANCE

back to the present day you. To make this clearer I will show you an example now using weight control as the focus, but you can adapt this idea to dealing with almost any problem.

I want to see yourself six months from now, you have been eating the right foods, healthy foods in the right amount to be fit and healthy and to be the weight that you want to be, see yourself now having made this change and actually being the weight you want to be, see yourself clearly and imagine how that feels to be this weight, the shape you want to be, now bring that feeling of achievement that good feeling back to the YOU of today, the YOU today who has made the decision to change the way you eat, this is the turning point, the moment of change, feel the good feeling that comes with that change. Now, if that YOU six months from now could speak to the YOU today, I wonder what they would say? I am guessing "thank you" might be the first thing, thank you for making the change and enabling me to be the weight I want to be, to empower me to control my weight, thank you, it feels good, you will feel how good this feels.....thank you, so that You six months from now is there, cheering you on and encouraging you, supporting you all the way with this change, as they cannot exist without you, they need you to make the change you are making today.

So you could use this technique to see yourself free of fear, free of anxiety, full of confidence, see yourself free from drinking alcohol, free from pain, you can use this for almost anything you want to change for yourself, using it to reinforce the changes you are making.

Planning your self-hypnosis session

The first thing we need to be clear about before you start a session of self-hypnosis is that you must not do this whilst driving or doing anything that requires your attention to keep you safe, such as operating machinery or even cooking. You need to be somewhere relatively quiet where you will be undisturbed for your session.

The next thing to do is to decide whether you are going to work quietly within your head or whether you want to prepare and record a session to listen to, whatever you do, the planning you put into the session will begin your therapy. At the end of the book there are some sample sessions to help guide you in constructing your sessions. When choosing what to put in the therapy it is like preparing a cake, different ingredients will give you different results and the previous sections have given you the generic ideas from which you can choose. Remember, it does not need to be complicated to be effective, but you may benefit from occasionally planning a more complex session, the point of self-hypnosis is that the choice is yours.

A non-recorded session

The best way to start is perhaps using the cue word approach, so choose your cue word, then look at the area you want to work with like anxiety or addiction and read through the ideas there and decide on what you feel most comfortable working with, some simple affirmations and direct suggestions may be best to start with, maybe adding a simple metaphor too. Write out these ideas fully so that you have a clear plan, go over it a few times so you have an idea of the process, then find a quiet moment and place to do your first practice. Keep all the notes you make for each session as you may want to go back and do the same session again sometime. If you are concerned you might drift off to sleep as you have had a busy day, you can always set a timer on your phone or an alarm of some sort to make sure you do not run over your allocated time, as stated before you will always become fully alert again, but if time is limited this precaution will give you peace of mind.

A recorded session

If you are recording a session for yourself, you can use more complex ideas and make the session longer. Always speak slowly and in a soft voice, you may want to experiment with your voice to get the tone and pace that feels right for you by just reading some of the inductions in the "getting into trance" section. If you want some ideas around how to pace your voice, you can listen to an example on my website.

To prepare your session, choose the induction you want to use, then go to the area of treatment and choose a selection of ideas, a metaphor, perhaps one of the techniques, some direct suggestions, affirmations and even some indirect suggestions, put them in an order that you feel flows, you then need to add in your way out of trance, perhaps a simple counting up from one to five, then type up your ideas or handwriting them to feel comfortable with the ideas, then all is ready and you can record your session. Before you start recording make sure the landline is off, alerts off on your mobile and that anyone in the house will leave you alone for a while. Recording the session should have some impact on your subconscious, however, once it is done take some quiet time to listen to it, daily if you can to really work with the change you want.

A simple breakdown for a recorded session

Induction

Metaphor

Direct suggestions/indirect suggestions

Future pacing

Affirmations

Come out of trance

Areas of Treatment

Addiction

About addiction

Addictive patterns of behaviours whether they are simply to chocolate, or something more damaging in the long term, such as alcohol or illegal drugs, are patterns that are locked in our subconscious mind, they are instinctive, and we barely take a second to process it in our conscious mind, we do not deliberately decide to do it, it has become an unconscious habit. The subconscious mind will provide the fuel for the addiction, feed it and fan it.

To fully understand addiction, we need to understand that it is the result of a habit, a habitual behaviour, but a habit can be a positive thing, our ability to drive for example is the result of a habitual response, when we first are learning to drive, we kept saying "mirror, signal, manoeuvre", until we were able to do it without consciously thinking about it, playing an instrument is just the same or indeed any skill we acquire like even being able to walk and talk. The capacity we have to learn something and make it a habit is useful, until it picks up a learning, a habit, that is bad for us, but we can turn it around, we need to take this ability to learn behaviour and introduce a new response, a new learning, re-framing the existing pattern and we can do this with hypnotherapy and self-hypnosis, as through this we can access those habitual behaviours in the subconscious mind.

Addictive behaviours are often the result of a response to anxiety and stress, providing the strategies for coping with the stress and strain of modern life is an essential part of the road to recovery, so if you want to try to help change an addictive pattern, look at your stress levels and work into your self-hypnosis some help for that too.

Many of our less helpful patterns are learned from our family, as that is how we learn about life, we learn to talk, we learn what is scary and we learn ways of coping with stress from the adults around us growing up, they give us our view of the world. Sometimes these patterns get reinforced by later events. However, the patterns got there, they are locked in our subconscious. By working on the patterns in the subconscious, whether they be learned from an adult as a child, or more instinctive responses to stress and anxiety, using self-hypnosis can help you to break that repetitive response.

We can utilise the ability to create an addiction to neutralise it, substituting alternative behaviours within the subconscious mind via a series of metaphors, metaphors and stories provide the link for the individual, the connecting strategies, links ideas together to provide the new behaviour. We can also use indirect and direct suggestions, embedded commands, then emphasise that change, building on your own imagination and creative response to lead to freedom from addiction. So, here are some ideas to help you.

Cutting the connection to addiction, any addiction.

This process will help cut your link, your connection to your addiction. It involves a visualisation process within trance that we can compare to a daydream, which we will use therapeutically. First read this process through, then choose the trance induction you want to use and work through it, then follow this visualisation process. You can do this all from memory or record it for yourself.

Use the power of your imagination to see two circles drawn on the ground touching each other like a giant number eight, the circles need to be large enough to see yourself standing in one of them.

Now you could imagine these circles painted on tarmac like you might see in a school playground, or painted on grass with white paint, or you might see them drawn in the sand or even as crop circles tramped down in the corn, use your imagination to create these circles.

Now imagine yourself in one of these two circles facing the other circle, so it is a giant figure of 8 drawn on the ground in some way and you are in one facing the other......now..... in the other circle put the focus of your addiction or a symbol of it....... so, if it is smoking you can put some packets of cigarettes.... or, pouches of tobacco in there, if it is alcohol some bottles or cans, for drugs put a stash as you would obtain it..... for gambling you could put a slot machine or a roulette wheel...... something that symbolises your addiction. It is in the other circle so you are protected from the influence of it, it cannot enter your circle.

Next you will see there is still something that connects you to whatever is in the other circle, it could be a piece of thread wrapped around the items in that circle and then going across the circle and wrapping itself around you....... I wonder if you can see this...... or a piece of rope...a chain.....it is wrapped around what is in the circle and linking it to you.... it cannot enter your circle but it is still affecting you in some way....... what we are going to do now will cut that connection........ break it once and for all so it can no longer affect you........ severing that connection....... so what you need to do now is to look around in your circle for whatever you need to cut that connection...... there may be some scissors there, shears, an axe, a knife or even some bolt cutters....... whatever it is that you need it is there, ready for you to use to cut that connection....... so now pick up what you have found which will be exactly what you need and cut it..... sever it..... break that connection to the addiction now, see that link, the tie break and now you are free to walk away from your circle and you are free from the influence of that addiction you have broken it at a deep level........deeper than your conscious......that's right, you have done it....... feel the relief sweeping through you.

You may want to repeat this exercise a few times to really get the impact of it, learning and change comes through repetition, it is how you gained the habit and you are applying similar principles to erase it.

Alcohol

Direct suggestion

I no longer need alcohol in my life, I have found a better way to do the things alcohol used to do for me, but does not do any more, I have found a new way, a way that do not hurt me and those close to me. What a relief that I do not need to keep drinking all that alcohol anymore.

Direct Suggestion 2

I have found a new way to do for me what alcohol used to do for me, but does not do now because I have found a better way to do it.

Indirect suggestion

I wonder at what point I will stop drinking alcohol today, will it be right away or an hour from now or maybe even two, I just wonder if I will even notice that I no longer have that urge to drink at the time I used to drink, but do not drink anymore.

Affirmation

I am no longer trapped by alcohol; I have a free choice I can choose to drink alcohol and I can choose not to drink alcohol; I am in control of my choices.

Alcohol is not ruling me any more

Metaphor - Alcohol - What's Your poison?

I wonder if you know that years ago when someone asked you what you wanted to drink….. an alcoholic drink….. they would say to

SELF-HELP? SELF-HYPNOSIS!

you "What's your poison"………. it was meant to be light hearted and funny……. people would chuckle away as they said it and then serve you a large dose of your poison. So, what is your poison? …..The poison that you choose….. as poison it is there is no doubt.

Can you imagine for a moment the effect that poison is having on your body…… sorry to press you on this…… but it is a poison…… so it is affecting your liver…… your pancreas that is struggling to process all that sugar…… in case you did not know…… just in case you did not know, that poison effects the communication between your brain and your body……. well you may have already experienced that, right?……..I mean just think what it must be doing to you when you cannot manage your movements properly or get your words out. ……What if someone said I want you to drink this?…… but afterwards you will not be able to walk straight and you might struggle to speak to me because your liver is drowning in the stuff and just cannot process it…… you might find your blood pressure shoots up……. it can affect your heart….. your lungs… ok I know, you have got the picture…… but if you really thought about it…… surely you would not down that poison in one…… if you really consider what it is. What's your poison?…. very funny……. I guess you might now know that your body can only process one unit of alcohol an hour…… no more than that and yes….. your liver is soaked in it….. drowning in the stuff……maybe you just might want to start making a decision about this poison…… maybe you might just want to think about what it is doing to you…….. never mind about what other people choose to do…. we are talking about you now….. if we really let your subconscious know….. that part of you that thinks this is ok….. let's let that part of your mind know what it is doing to you…… maybe it did not realise in the way it does now…… maybe now is the time to find a new way a better way to do whatever it is you think alcohol is doing for you right now, a way that does not damage and hurt you, surely now that you know you would not deliberately do that to you, would you? Would you really, really take on that poison?…..maybe it would help your mind to see the poison symbol…..you may have seen it on TV or on a chemical bottle somewhere……. see that symbol…… you know that skull and crossbones symbol, seeing it there, whenever you see a bottle of alcohol, seeing that symbol there so at least you remember….. at least you cannot kid yourself anymore, danger of death it says……. that is what poisons do, so whatever your poison is, you will not see it in the same way as before……….. you cannot see it in the same way as before now that you know…….. so now you know what you are no longer going to do to you…

Smoking

Direct suggestion

I no longer need to smoke cigarettes as that was a decision of my younger self, who did not care for my health and I have quite literally changed my mind about smoking, as I have changed my mind about other things in the past, I am a non-smoker now, what a relief to know I no longer need to breathe in all those poisons.

Indirect suggestion

"I wonder if I will stop smoking right now, right this minute, I wonder if that was my last cigarette or if I will have just one more cigarette before I stop altogether."

"What a relief that I no longer need to smoke anymore"

Affirmation

I am a non-smoker for the rest of my life.

I am no longer a person who smokes cigarettes.

I feel no need, no craving to smoke any more.

Metaphor – Smoking - Fresh Air

Do I really need to point out to you the importance of the air that you breathe? ……..from that very first breath to your very last……

it is that air you need to sustain your very life…….. that oxygen that powers your body….. the air…….the air is vital to you…… just mentioning it in case for some reason it had passed you by…… as why oh why would you choose to pollute that air….. I mean, we are working so hard to keep the air clean!

They stopped open fires in London decades ago to stop all that polluting smoke clogging up the skies and then there is the clean emissions policies and congestion charges to keep the air clean in cities around the world and you……..you choose to deliberately pollute the air you breath in…. sucking the smoke in…… the tar….. coating your lungs with it……. ok, I know your conscious mind may have woken up to the fact this is not a great idea…….but let's get your subconscious involved, as that is the part of you that has been enforcing this decision that I am guessing you made many years ago…… years ago when you did not care perhaps what happened to you…… could not catch a glimpse of your mortality….. well I am showing you that mortality now……you need to clean out those tarred up lungs and take care of you now and go for the clean air….. clean emissions thing……. you have changed your mind about the decision you made all that while ago and we are telling your subconscious now that you want to stop……stop polluting the air that you breathe…… stop gassing yourself, and take care of you now and if you thought for some reason that breathing in all this smoke actually calmed you down….. well that is all an illusion….. it actually pushes the heart rate faster….well you do not need me to tell you anymore that smoking can kill you……. I guess you have known that for a while….. but what about your subconscious….. let's give it a chance to get on board and stop….. stop smoking…….. stop poisoning the air that you breathe.

Gambling

Direct suggestion

I no longer want to throw my money away, waste it, lose it, I do not want to be a loser any more, I want to be a winner, winning matters to me so I do not choose to gamble anymore because it creates losers, I do not want to lose any more. I focus my desire to win on something I can do, rather than on something where I am set up to be the loser.

Indirect suggestion

Quitting gambling is not something that I will not find easy now.

Affirmation

I no longer feel the need to gamble. I feel no need, no craving to gamble.

Gambling is no longer a part of my life.

I leave gambling in the past.

Metaphor - Gambling - Doors

You are in a long corridor and there are two doors ahead of you...... one on the left and one on the right hand side...... you need to pick one of these doors...... it is an important decision and it is hard to know which door to pick, then you notice there is a tiny spy hole in each door...... so you go up to the left hand door and you look inside....... in there you see yourself three years from now, you look a bit older...... you can see time is not being very kind to you, your face looks strained.....you are alone it seems there is no one around you..... no sign of any family past or present, you seem to be just sitting on your own in the room....... it is a shabby room, your clothes look scruffy, there does not seem to be anything left of any value in the room, it is not a room you recognise......you might have thought you did at first, but it looks more like a rough bedsit...... you wonder how it could have come to this, this is not the life that you want...... then you hear this You..... this You inside the room talking and you put your ear to the door to hear....... you hear the words "why did I not stop, why did I keep thinking there was a winner around the next corner?...... why did I not challenge this and find a different way to do for me, what the gambling used to do?...... Did I want thrills and excitement?...... What did I want?.... How could I have got it another way?.......Is there any way out of this place?..... What have I done?..... What have I not done?.... What a loser I must look and there was me expecting to be a winner.......I have lost count of the losses now"

You pull back not wanting to hear and see any more..... You go to the right hand door..... you look through the peep hole there..... you see yourself three years from now..... not looking really any older..... looking relaxed...... in a nice home....... there are possessions there that you treasure and do not want to lose..... there are people around you..... family and friends, you can see by your expression on your face that you are contented...... settled, safe, yes safe and that looks like a pretty good thing....... you can see that you are talking, you press your ear to the door "what a relief that I am not controlled any more, I am not being pushed around and bullied by that urge...... that I am free from that habit now, that I fought it, that I found a new way to do for me....... what the gambling used to do for me and does not do now, because I have found a different way, I dare not even think about where I would be now if I had not, not broken the pattern...I am not a loser anymore" You pull back from the door, now brace yourself, it is time to make that choice........ ask that deep part of your mind to help you with the decision, to help you on that next step....... open the door and step inside.

Food Addiction

Direct suggestion

I am no longer that person that overeats, I have no need, no craving and no desire to overeat any more.

Indirect

I do not need to tell myself not to overeat any more, as not overeating is not something I will not find easy now.

Affirmation

I eat the amount of food I need to be fit and healthy.

Metaphor - Food issues - Fuel up!

We seem to have gone very wrong, with our relationship with food....we either have too much and hurt ourselves that way or starve ourselves....as a sign of control.....reacting to social pressures........or what....so hard to always know......but whether it is too much food ....or not enough food........we seem to have forgotten food is the fuel for our bodies....we need air......... we need water........we need food.......we need these things to live.....we do not have a distorted relationship with the air.....or with water.....but with food.......now here is the thing....if we stop glamorising it......if we just see it as fuel for our body.... maybe we can think that ....not enough food and eventually we will grind to a halt......too much food.....overloaded with food.... well, if it were your car.......you would have flooded the carburettor and it would still not move...still stuck....unable to do what you need it to do.........so let's get back to the idea......the very basic idea that food is the fuel for our body and we need it........but we need the right fuel....and enough fuel......let your subconscious mind take this on board....reframe the relationship....your relationship with food......thinking about food in this new way...giving it the attention it deserves to give you life.......but then getting on with your life.........giving it a new perspective........keeping it in perspective.......eating the food that you need to be healthy and well......taking care of you now......as you would maintain....service and MOT your car...... maintaining your body weight...to the right weight......eating...... fuelling up...the right amount....see it as a tank that needs enough to get you to your next destination but needing enough....... getting in tune with what your body actually needs...the fuel it needs.......your subconscious is going to understand and process what I say in a new way....and I wonder when you will notice the new awareness...hearing my voice in your head saying food is fuel.......fuel up.......but fuel up right....that's right.......

Metaphor - Food issues - Gastric band

I wonder when you will notice that you just cannot eat the amount of food that you did before....will you notice before you start eating?....or will you notice as you eat ....how quickly you feel that full feeling...that feeling as if you have been eating for hours....because your stomach is so much smaller than before......it is constricted and constrained....held in check by that band........it is such a simple operation...quick and swift.....to just put in that restriction to divide your stomach in two....that is what they do.......you may have forgotten that you had it done......but there it is......you can feel it.....that full feeling so quickly whenever you eat......you cannot fit any more in than a cup of food at a time... as it needs to pass through such a narrow tube.....allow it to pass right through...not overloading the system as the food passes safely through the spaces provided, filling the small space provided and that is what you decided to do.....that is why the gastric band is there....can you feel the tightness I wonder when you eat your food...as it holds you in check....creating a small space for you to fill...then you get that full feeling.......I know you know what I mean.....so from now on......just a few mouthfuls of food and the space is so small...that will be enough......no more room in there........so you will have to wait until the next mealtime......like having a tight belt on around your waist.....holding you back from allowing more food in.......no room in there.....no room at the inn........can you feel it I wonder.....the restriction there...that means you eat a little at a time......taking care of you.....taking care not to stretch and to strain the small stomach in there.....no more room.....so you need to think about what you put in......as the space is so small you need to get the right nourishment in.....no space for cakes and biscuits you need to save the room in there for the nutrition you need.....how good it feels to use that space wisely...the space provided...to store up the energy you need....the nutrition you need.....to be healthy and strong.....you might even want to imagine the small space provided......the band in there....like a tight belt holding it in.......so now you have taken this step....this step of change.....you may to even notice, noticing at first that you are putting less in.......because there is less space provided and you can judge what to do......though you may notice perhaps just from time to time....that tight feeling that lets you know so much more swiftly than before, that you are full, so very full after a few mouthfuls of food....enough food to remain fit and healthy.....but no more overload....no risk of exploding through overloading the system in there like the pressure cooker.......take the pressure off......eating just enough food..... the right food....not wasting that space with fatty and sweet foods.....as these do not nourish you.....fuelling up with the healthy food you need in the small space in there......

Metaphor - Food issues - The Furnace

I want to talk to you about how you fuel your body ....and how your body utilises that fuel, firstly the food you eat...... the food you choose to eat is the fuel you need to power your body....... your body needs this fuel to work efficiently.......... when you eat that food....... when you put it into your body.... the healthy food....the right kind of food......... you burn that fuel up............ to power your mind and your body.......... I would like you to think about that now........ the furnace in your body that burns the fuel and turns it into energy for you......... I wonder if you have seen in an old film, or in real life a steam engine when the stoker puts coal into the furnace......... it creates the steam that powers the engine....your body has a similar system .... I would like to imagine it now.......... that furnace burning up the fuel you put into it..............but of course we need to consider the kind of fuel you put into your body........... you want the right kind of fuel.........that steam engine needs coal to fuel it........... if you put a pile of ordinary stones in there they would sit there in the furnace getting hotter ....so first thing you need is the right kind of fuel for your body......... thinking as you rest there now about the right fuel to put in........not fatty or sugary foods, they will not give you the energy you need and they will not burn properly just like those lumps of stone in the furnace……….so selecting the right fuel for your body now……….leaving the fat and the sugar and eating healthy foods that your furnace can burn swiftly and efficiently and ………..now we can watch that furnace with the right foods in there and it is burning that fuel up quickly and converting it into the energy you need…………… I would like you to use that powerful mind of yours to see this happening now……….. and there is a dial on the outside of your furnace and you can turn it right up to full power………..so that furnace that processes your fuel is working at peak performance…………and I wonder if you notice that if you try to cheat your body and sneak in the wrong kind of food……….. the wrong kind of fuel……..it is slow to process and you know that your body is not happy and to speed everything up, you need the right fuel ………and turn that dial up and ……….feel the processing speed up ……… your metabolism increase……… seeing that steam-train propelled through the countryside………speeding up and racing along in just the same way your body will feel ……… you will burn off that fat and you feel better day by day ………..as you take care of you now and your body has speeded up, burning off the fat……… chasing away the fat as you accelerate ahead, doing what you need to do for you now.

One thing to make clear you are not going on a diet…..I am not suggesting a diet……..you are changing your patterns once and for all……..a diet is transient……a diet passes……….a diet is a temporary reprieve for your body………..now you are changing the way you fuel your body……changing the way you eat….. retiring from eating the wrong kind of food…retiring from treating your body like a dumping ground for all sorts of things that are bad for it…changing your patterns once and for all….taking care of you now…..what a relief to know…that furnace that powers your body can work properly now……efficiently now….so efficiently now…..working quickly…powering your mind and your body…..your body works better now…your mind thinking more clearly now because it has the right kind of food now.

Anger

About anger

Anger is an overwhelming emotion. It is linked to the stress response that we have already discussed, in particular the fight part, the anger fuels the self-protective fight element of the fight/flight/freeze response as a defensive strategy. Whilst experiencing this, all empathy and compassion needs to be buried deep, to enable survival in the fight, as if you were in a real danger situation, you could not afford to have any positive feeling towards your opponent, or it would put you at risk. This is why when you are angry at someone whom in ordinary circumstances you love, it is as if they have become someone else, someone you do not know, because your subconscious needs you to have no sympathy with them to enable your perceived survival. You need to distance yourself from them and any positive emotional connection you might have, or if it were a real case of survival you would not survive as you would supress your most ruthless side. It is hard to rationalise with someone when they are gripped by anger, because at a subconscious level they are fighting to protect themselves and survive. I wonder if you have noticed a time when someone you love who would ordinarily go to great lengths to support you and contribute to your happiness is all of a sudden, behaving differently, like an enemy, your worst enemy. Maybe you have experienced a feeling like this when suddenly someone you love becomes someone to be attacked and despised? Yet, if something bad were to happen to them when you felt like this, the anger would quickly dissipate, because it has been created as an artificial protection, it will vanish and the original emotion return, but perhaps accompanied by some guilt and confusion at how you had temporarily lost those positive feelings.

Anger is not always expressed through shouting and outward signs of aggression, it can be repressed and come out in more indirect ways such as a withdrawal of attention, or forms of subtle manipulation and bullying. Sometimes the anger will be directed at a weaker opponent than the original cause, like someone who is angry with their boss but comes home and picks a fight with their partner, this is called displacement and is very common. Sometimes we can even be angry at ourselves for something, but blame someone else for it, perhaps even accusing them of even behaving exactly like you have done, we call this projection.

When anger is in full spate it is hard to even think clearly, as is with stress, blood flow is diverted from the cognitive thinking part of the brain into the primal survival part of the brain.

One of the first things you can do with your own anger, is to begin to start to notice when it arrives, you might feel it arriving first in your body somewhere and feel that red mist creeping into your mind, start to notice the very moment it begins and keep that noticing, that will be the beginning of change for you. Then just begin to question the anger, begin to isolate the real reason for it. If it is hard in the moment, take some time after the event to examine your anger, give it a reality check, give it some real perspective. Did the situation warrant the level of your response? Could it be that the perceived initial object of your anger was not the cause of the anger at all? Are you catastrophizing and getting a situation out of perspective and is this a pattern? Keep an anger journal and begin to notice the patterns, times and causes, so you can begin to understand what is really happening for you and this will help you to address the real rather than initially perceived causes. When you find yourself slipping into that swirling pool of anger, just try to slow it down a little, give your mind time to process what is really going on here rather than dealing with that in the aftermath. If we begin to understand our anger and what is fuelling it, when we start to confront it, we can begin, just begin to dilute it.

Visualisation exercise for anger

Think about a situation when you have been angry recently and imagine clearly in your mind the location you were in, the room or outside space, see the colours and the shapes around you, make it as clear as you can, now see yourself in this situation and anyone else who was involved in this angry situation. I want you to watch as if you were a spectator, an observer, a passer-by, you are not participating in this, you are just watching. Perhaps you could imagine you have gone back in a time machine and you are just visiting this past event as an observer. What are you wearing, can you remember? How do the other people/the other person look? What is/are their facial expressions? How does your face look? What can you hear in this situation? Are there sounds other than voices? Think about what you can hear. Now, hone-in on the voices, what are you saying? Can you remember what you said? Can you see your expression as you said it? Can you see it now? What about anyone else involved. What are they saying? I want you to watch this scene and see how it looks and sounds. How does it feel to watch this? If you could press the pause button on this scene and rewind it, I would like you to think about how you would have done this differently now, with all that you know now, just take some time to look at this scene and maybe change the expression on your face, alter the words, see it pan out differently, you have watched the scene and now, now you are going to re-write the scene, like a director of a stage play, now tell the characters what you want them to do and see this all playing out differently, give yourself time to do this now.

You can do this exercise whenever you feel a situation has got out of control and the more you observe and re-run your actions, particularly if you do so relaxed in a gentle trance, the easier it will be for you to change your responses in the future, the very act of observation will impact on future behaviour. You do not have to be in a trance to do this exercise, but if you can relax the mind a little it will enhance the benefit.

Direct suggestions for anger

What purpose does this anger have for me right now? what is it doing for me? maybe it feels it is protecting me, if it is protecting me, what is it protecting me from? Why do I need protecting? Is my anger the best way to protect me in this situation? Can I find another way to protect myself in this situation? Am I in any real danger? Or is this just perceived danger? What else can do for me, what my anger has been doing for me but is not going to do now as I have decided I can find better ways to achieve this?

My anger does not just hurt others but it hurts me too and I no longer want to do things that hurt me, I want to protect me and the best way to protect me is to find another way to protect me and leave the anger in the past, behind me in the past with the other things I used to do, but do not do any more as they are hurtful to me. I am free from anger now, it is a past part of me, I leave this part of me in the past, how good it feels to know I do not need this anger any more, what an incredible relief.

Indirect suggestion for anger

I wonder if I try not to notice when that anger just snuffs out like a candle guttering out when your back is turned, just snuffed out without me noticing that the moment has passed and that a calm peace is returning to me, the firework lying spent on the ground, the moment has passed.

Metaphor - Fanning the flames

A fire starts from a spark..... a spark that has to be fanned and encouraged to survive.... I wonder if you have ever seen fire start in the old fashioned way by rubbing two sticks together...... the smoke rises...... then there is the spark which you blow upon to sustain it, then feed it with materials that will burn and it will burst into fire....... real fire not just a spark....... but you have to keep fanning the flames.......encouraging them........ you have to keep feeding the fire to keep it alight and it needs oxygen to survive, so many things in place to keep the fire burning....... I would like to suggest to you that your anger is just like that fire, starting from a small spark..... a flare of anger...... but you have to sustain that anger to keep it there....... fan it with your attention...... feeding it with new reasons........ new ideas of why it is justified..... why you have a right to feel it?....... all that self-justification for your anger.......feeding it and making it flare...... of course you have the choice to remove your attention from it and stop fanning the flames of it, stop nursing that anger into life, stop coaxing that anger into existence.

I wonder if you can catch it when it is just a spark......just beginning...... or whether it will have truly caught before you stop the anger......... before you withdraw your attention from it and it fizzles out and I wonder if you have noticed when you have left that anger behind, there are times in the past when you have known that feeling.......that angry feeling and now you know that feeling has passed...... it is in the past and how you cannot reignite it........ in fact sometimes it is hard to remember just how you managed to create such a massive fire from such a small spark....... but now you know you have snuffed it out, you could even imagine....... more than withdrawing your attention and no longer fanning the flames of it, you could see yourself throwing a bucket of water over it and completely snuffing it out...... best way to be sure...... to be sure of leaving it in the past where it belongs. I wonder when you will notice that moment has passed....... right away or a few minutes from now, that you notice the fire has gone out.

Affirmations

Anger is no longer a part of my life.

I am calm in situations where I would have been angry before.

I feel no anger.

I will not be governed by anger any more.

Anger hurts me as much as it hurts others.

Anxiety

About Anxiety

Anxiety is not something we deliberately choose to experience, we understand that now, as we have looked at the stress response, the control mechanism that creates anxiety and panic attacks. That stress response releases the shot of adrenalin into the system and then all our body functions swing into action to support the need to fight, to run or to freeze. But we need to keep in mind that the physical shot of adrenalin that sets you into your anxious state has a short shelf life, it will have been triggered by your subconscious through a perceived threat, but then the conscious mind gets involved. Your conscious mind recognises the fear response and often it begins to stoke and provoke the fear, it sets up an internal dialogue that often magnifies the fear and keeps that stress response flooding the body system with chemicals. By taking control of these wild conscious thoughts, we can begin to control that stress response and stop it from feeding the anxiety. Through improved thought processing and relaxation exercises in self-hypnosis we will have much fewer moments of unconscious anxiety and better control in the conscious, but even if that reaction has begun, you can do something to stop it and prevent it spiralling out of control, knowing and understanding that is the first step to change.

I use many metaphors to describe this feeling of anxiety when it starts and some may resonate with you such as a runaway train, after all we say train of thought, but sometimes that train feels like it is heading off into places we really do not want to go. We can consider the idea of thoughts like wild horses, racing and chasing, but wild horses can be tamed with applied skill and sometimes even visualising yourself mounting one of the horses wrestling with it to slow it down, can be enough to distract the mind from the original concern and give you a sense of control back. The nature of those repetitive thoughts, like a hamster turning around and around on a wheel can be stopped and there are many different techniques that you can use. The main approach is not to fight the fear thoughts, not to try in the moment of the fear to reason with them, but to just shift the focus of your attention, you can fan the flames of the anxiety by giving it all of your attention or you can withdraw your attention from it and it will fizzle out like a fire starved of oxygen. A lot of the exercises I will recommend to you are to divert you from promoting the anxiety thoughts.

Anxiety is probably one of the largest problems we face in life as we are bombarded through so many kinds of media now with information that feeds fear and worry, often with things that are beyond our control to have any influence on, like issues in the wider world and we have our own concerns too, like financial security, relationship issues and health problems which may be escalating due to our anxiety and stress. The first thing to recognise in any situation is that if we cannot control an outcome, worrying about it will not actually change that outcome, this may seem a simple statement but one we rarely acknowledge if we can find a true acceptance of it at a subconscious level, it will make you a calmer person.

We often catastrophise situations blowing them out of proportion, just bringing in a gentle questioning at these moments when in a light trance can bring in a reality check. Consider the following:

"Does this situation really warrant this level of fear?"

"Have I survived something similar before?"

"How dangerous is this situation really to me?"

"Am I in real danger right now?"

If the situation does not require the level of fear, if you have survived such a situation before, if the situation is not of real danger then we can begin to get the system to stand down from ready for action and perhaps instead of imagining all the results of the situation you are in as negative, we can take an alternative approach and visualise them turning out well, because we do have a choice, or if we have no choice, we have a choice of how we respond to it. There are many things in our lives that are out of control, but I would like to remind you that one thing you can absolutely take control of are the many thoughts in your head as it is you that put them there, you are tolerating them being there and encouraging them to stay.

There are other metaphors in this book that may help with anxiety, such as the metaphors under the depression section and the cinema technique in the phobia section.

Direct suggestion

I can keep provoking my anxiety by thinking about it, by chasing it around in my mind, or I can choose to stop and right now I am making a decision to stop, to stop fuelling the anxiety and taking my attention to a different source of thought, because I know I face choices at each and every moment and my choice now is to stop the anxiety by thinking of something that reminds me of feeling good instead. I can challenge that thought, if the thought that makes me anxious has no other purpose than to make me anxious then I tell it to stop, I choose something else, a good memory, a good feeling, I can switch the anxiety off and I know I can do it because I switched it on in the first place, so I can make it stop, how empowering to realise that I can delete what I have created, switch if right off...

Indirect suggestion

I wonder if I will notice noticing the moment that the anxiety stops, the very moment when I feel calm again, when calm and comfortable thoughts replace that anxiety, will I notice it straight away or five minutes afterwards or five minutes after that, it is interesting to wonder at what point the anxiety stops and I notice noticing that the moment has passed.

Metaphor - Spinning top

The mind can feel like it is spinning around and around when you feel anxious….. spinning out of control…… perhaps you can see a spinning top…… going around and around……. you perhaps did this when you were a child…… put the spinning top on a steady surface and gave it a strong twirl and around and around it goes……. but if you want it to keep spinning you have to keep applying more spin to the top…….. you have to keep topping it up, like a spinning plate in the air it takes work to keep it there…… anxiety can feel like this too, spinning around in your head……. but you have to keep working at it to keep it there, provoking it with new thoughts, the thoughts going over and over around and around…….. if you leave it alone it will stop…….. just like the spinning top……. let it go, let it slow and it will stop spinning, fall onto its side and sway a little from side to side and then it stops……. what a relief to let it stop, stop making that top spin…….. just leave it alone for a while……. take your mind and apply it to a different job….. and the top will stop……..the anxiety will fade slowly winding down until it rocks slightly and then it stops……. and you can let it stop……..give yourself permission to let it stop…

Metaphor - Dials

Imagine a control room in your mind with all the dials showing all the different settings for your functions in your body and your mind….. there is one for your body temperature set nicely in the middle not too hot not too cold……. one for your heart rate it might be a little fast so let's set the rhythm now….. to a nice steady rhythm…. feeling your heart now at a nice steady beat, there is one for your breathing…… taking control, seeing that symbol that shows the air coming in and out of your body rise gently up and down, breathing in and out, like the ebb and flow of the tide lapping the shore......... in and out, a natural steady flow, aware now of that natural flow in and out....... how about your anxiety levels right now, I should imagine they are dropping but let's take a look...... seeing the dial for that in front of you, there is the needle pointing to high, but it is dropping down now....... you can take control of it.........I wonder if you can imagine taking hold of that dial and turning it down......... turning the anxiety levels down........ I wonder if you can notice the relief as you see the pointer on the dial....... it moves down to low........ right at the bottom of the dial......... breathing out a sigh of relief....... as the needle settles on low and you feel a wave of calm flowing through you....... that is all it takes to focus your mind for a moment...... take control in the moment and turn the anxiety dial down and your body releases all the relaxing chemicals into your bloodstream and everything slows right down........ what a relief to know that you know now how to take control in this way and see everything slowing down a peaceful slowing down now........ using the power of your subconscious mind to take control of your body........ so peaceful now you would have to work hard to generate that anxiety now as you have found the pleasure of the calm feeling.......why would you want that stress feeling back when you can choose this peaceful feeling, can you not?

Metaphor - Intrusive thoughts – Spam Filter

There are those thoughts you do not want....... they might worry you or scare you...... or suggest you do something that does not seem right to you....something you do not want to do....... and you worry away at it.......... let it take over your mind........ until there is no room for any other thought.....well, I see it like this, when you check your emails..... you will see a list appear all jostling for your attention....... now when you see those ones that are clearly junk........stuff perhaps your spam filter has missed...... you do not waste the time reading them through........ the spam..... the rubbish......the stuff that is not relevant to you........ or even that might damage your computer as it has a virus in..........you just delete it right away........ not saving it for another day……. or perhaps we could look at it another way…….. as the post plops through the letterbox……. you know which are the letters……… which are the bills……..which is the stuff to through away…..the circulars……. the advertising for things you do not want or need…… you do not give yourself special time to read it all through…..the junk…….. just gets thrown into the bin as you give your attention to what needs it first……selecting the letter……or the urgent email and leaving the junk behind……. well those unwanted thoughts……. those intrusive thoughts…. they are just junk of sorts…… not needed…… not wanted….. so just discard it when it comes….. delete it……setting up your own internal spam filter I guess…… even say in your head this is junk I do not want it……..what shall I focus on instead……just delete before reading, no need to give it your attention now…….. so when it arrives now, just choosing a different source of thought instead………. and as you receive this thought now…….. both parts of your mind can feel the relief and the knowing that you can just let it go……..what a relief to know you do not need to give it your attention……. let it go……. along with other unwanted rubbish….that's right…choosing a different thought…. something that makes you feel good instead of bad….you can do that now, can you not?……..

Affirmations

I release the anxiety.

I am not my anxiety. It does not define me.

Anxiety no longer controls me, I control my anxiety.

Confidence

About confidence

To have confidence is to have belief in ourselves and our abilities which comes from our sense of self, self-worth, self-esteem. Many people suffer from a lack of confidence which can affect all areas of life and usually starts in childhood, we are not born with self-doubt and fear, it is something that we learn from our experiences. Lack of confidence can come from many different causes, let's look at some of them. A child does not have the filter to assess the validity of criticism and takes generalised statements as true, such as, a child might spill their drink on the carpet and they are told "you are a bad child" and they believe they are bad, they cannot evaluate that making a simple mistake is not enough to make them bad and if they hear it regularly enough then it becomes a fixed belief, remember we learn by repetition, so growing up in a critical family atmosphere will have an impact on future mental health. Children want their parents to be pleased with them and will often work hard for that attention and praise, for whatever reason some parents withhold the praise and then the child will feel whatever they do is not good enough and will carry this feeling into adult life, sometimes within families there is a lot of competition for adult attention and those that get the least will have much lower confidence levels. Sometimes a small event like being laughed at when trying to do something, particularly in our impressionable school days, can leave its mark and we are unable to overcome the fear of being observed and judged by others, who may in fact be no better, cleverer or more skilled than us. Often bullies at school or at work are just attacking others to mask their own inadequacies but can leave lasting problems that can be carried right through life if we do not deal with them. We are also able to create low confidence ourselves through perceived failure, such as criticising ourselves for not doing something well enough, we are often our harshest critics and expect to excel at something when we may have little experience in it, it is important to allow ourselves time to learn and develop to gain confidence. Whatever the cause of low confidence, self-hypnosis can be a powerful way to change self-perception. You may also find it useful if you are struggling with low confidence to read the section on resilience too.

Impact of Social Media on Confidence

Advertising one's life on social media is feeding into people's low self-esteem issues and enhancing existing problems. How we look has become even more important with young women and girls posting images of themselves and having to conform to current perceived views of beauty. There is a lot of cyber bullying, as people seem to feel able to say things on social media that they would never say to someone's face and the harshness of some comments which are out there in the public domain for anyone to see, can be extremely damaging whether the criticism is aimed at appearance, skills or even perceived lack of friends. People are also being affected by seeing others constantly bragging about their own successes, supposedly perfect relationships and perfect children and anyone with any confidence issues seeing this will sink down even further as they feel their lives are not living up to expectation. The world has become a place of very public fierce competition in which many fail to thrive. For anyone sensitive to this the first vital step is to take yourself out of the social media environment and keep to the input of real rather than perceived friends. It is important to learn to be more private again.

Low confidence effects

The effects of low self-confidence can lead to social anxiety disorders, difficulty in forming relationships and poor performance in the work environment, panic attacks, depression and in critical cases suicide, so it is a serious problem and the earlier we begin to examine and try to boost confidence levels the better for long term mental health and well-being.

Modelling

An idea called modelling is often utilised within Hypnosis and NLP (Neuro-Linguistic Programming) to help develop a positive skill. We learn many of our patterns and behaviours from our parents and the people around us as we grow up, we have no other template for life, they give us their version of life, this is not always helpful to us, sometimes needs to be adapted and changed. We have this skill to copy another person, if you watch a young child with a parent it can be entertaining to see that mimicry. We can utilise this early skill to build our confidence and develop skills. We just need to find someone who does what we want to do well and observe them, see how they do it, their body language, attitude, verbal language and tone, by doing this and then copying it we can be as they are. "Fake it until you make it" may be a term you have heard before and this is something you may have actually done before, but not realised it, particularly young people will want to fit into their peer groups and unconsciously copy those around them, now you can use this skill in a conscious way, for a positive result.

Utilising Modelling for confidence

Imagine someone whom you see as confident, just picture them in your mind, or if visualising things is not comfortable for you, just think about this person, it could be someone that you know or someone you have seen on the television, think about them, think about how they walk, how they stand, how they use their body language, their hands, their arms, think about the kind of words that they use and their tone of voice, how they sound when they are talking, focus in on them in your mind. I wonder if you could see inside their mind what sort of things that they say to themselves, what is their inner dialogue? Think about what it is they do, that makes them appear confident to you.

I would like you to imagine them in a situation you would like to be confident in, see them handling the situation well, how do they stand, walk, talk, what are they saying and doing in this situation, see it in your mind as if you were watching it play out on the stage, watch them dealing with this for you, think about how they would deal with this for you, now imagine floating into them on the stage and imagine dealing with the situation just like them, you are playing a part, you are playing the part of them playing your part on the stage, feel how much easier it is to be them doing what needs to be done, I wonder how it feels to be just like them, like being an actor on the stage you can play this part and be just like them, how does it feel to be just like them and handle this situation so well? How does it feel to see this situation turning out well? You can take this ability to be just like them in any situation you face, imagine it in your mind see what they would do and how they would do it and play the part and soon, very soon you will find you do not have to think about it at all, this ability to do things well, to do things confidently will become a part of you, seeing yourself clearly thinking and doing just as they do, calm and confident, so very calm and confident now. Seeing future situations and how they go differently now because you do what they do, act as they do, appear confident as they do.

We are now going to look at something called the law of association and just see how it can help you with confidence and many other things too.

Law of Association and Anchoring

The law of association is the link between a psychological state-thought, how you feel in simple terms to an outside stimulus which could be a sight, smell, sound or touch. It is this stimulus, this outside thing that leads to your emotional or psychological response. The scientist Pavlov in 1897 devised an experiment known as the "Pavlov's Dogs" experiment, whereby he rang a bell every time he fed his dogs, he then discovered that every time he rang a bell the dogs would salivate expecting food, they had begun to associate the bell with food. It is known as Pavlovian conditioning/classical conditioning and gives us the law of association. In this experiment we describe the bell as an "anchor" as it is the bell that is triggering the response in the dogs.

I am sure we have all experienced this, a perfume will remind you of a particular person which may be a good or a bad association, a song can bring on an associated happy or sad feeling, this sound linking into our emotional state and recreating it, the smell of bread baking might make you think of your grandmother's kitchen, so we have had experiences where how we feel, has an outside trigger. We can find these associations are positive or negative, many of our fears come from triggers and associations, thus we need to replace a negative trigger with a positive one, that we can turn to when needed.

Milton Erickson, a renowned psychologist and hypnotherapist, took this idea one stage further and said that our senses are linked to our emotions. Thus, through using anchoring in hypnosis we can directly influence those emotions, particularly if we use the memory of our senses to enhance the experience.

It may be useful to begin to notice situations which make you feel uncomfortable, more nervous and see if there is a common denominator to these as there may be a negative trigger there that you need to be aware of, to then neutralise it with a positive one. A diary of feelings can be useful to track down our positive and negative triggers, we need to know the things that are triggering our bad feelings, it is equally useful to know what turns on the positive ones so we can emphasise those more.

How to utilise hypnotic anchoring:

We can create a positive association, anchor or trigger to feel more confident, we can also use it to feel less anxious or to tackle certain fears. For example, associating touching a particular place on the hand with feeling confidence or feeling calm and safe, will create a safe anchoring point. We can do this whilst creating a confident feeling through one of the exercises like the modelling one above, or other confident suggestions and metaphors and when you have created that good feeling, touch the place on your hand, so it becomes the link through to this confident feeling. Many people will just touch their first finger and thumb together to link through to that better feeling, but you need to do it when you are relaxed in trance to really tap into that good feeling, we will look at it in more detail below. We can also tap into good feelings to feel calmer and more relaxed by focusing on a happy memory, an experience or even focusing on a place that makes us feel relaxed and happy, then touching the place on your hand to create your new anchor/trigger.

Using an anchor for confidence

Imagine a situation when you have achieved something that made you feel good about yourself, if possible, see it as a picture in your mind, see the colours, focus in on any sounds you can associate with this experience, if there are any touch sensations you can associate with this experience imagine them, revisit the memory as if you were really there and allow the good feelings to be present, there may be sounds that you associate with this experience too, use all your senses to make this strong for you. Now anchor these good feelings for yourself in any way that feels right for you, you might want to put your thumb and forefinger together, or press any two fingers together, place your hand on your side, or any physical gesture that will link your mind into this experience. Whenever you need to feel confident in any situation, use this previous memory of you doing something well and it does not matter how different the experience was, use your anchoring method to bring the good feelings to the surface and feel the confidence surge through you, just like turning on a power source, or opening a tap, you could even visualise this confident energy flowing through you when you need it, as soon as you use your trigger/anchor.

Challenging your beliefs about yourself – Reality check

Sometimes we build a sense of low self-esteem or low worth from just a single event or someone saying something to us at an impressionable time. We then build the story of the image of oneself from this and it gets bigger and bigger and has a more powerful hold over us over time. For example, we might say "I am useless" so repeatedly that we believe it and that belief makes us less able to do things effectively, what we believe becomes a reality. We call these kind of statements "generalisations". We need to look for when that generalised view of yourself began. It may be that we were asked a question in class at school and were unable to answer, people then teased you for not answering and the story of being useless begins, it may be there are many other subjects you are brilliant at, just not this one thing where you failed to perform, but you focus entirely on the failure. It may be that those that teased you did not know the answer either and their teasing was to cover up their own low self-esteem. By creating this story of uselessness, we are actually distorting reality and we need to challenge that distortion, so it is important to try to find out how the story has begun, but first I will share with you a story of mine.

I had an experience where I developed a faulty story which I often use as an example in my work. I had to be filmed on camera and as I liked public speaking, I thought I would be good at it, but when the moment came, I fluffed my lines and was not very good, I had never done it before but expected to be instantly good at it. So after that first time, I always said, "I am no good on camera" I said it so often that when the time came for me to have to do it again, I was so convinced of my failure, I was even worse than before and the story got even bigger. It was only when I became a therapist that I realised what I had done, creating my own failure repeatedly from just one experience. I worked on challenging this belief, I looked at where it began, told myself that to base a belief about myself on just two experiences was not realistic and that I needed to try again and not expect myself to be perfect instantly at it and that I would get better, rather like when we learn to walk we have to fall down a few times before we get it right and then I tried it again, I was much better and though may never be brilliant at it, I could do it and do it competently.

Let us look at how to challenge the story you have created about the things you do not believe you are good at, or other generalised negative beliefs. So, relax yourself comfortably into a trance state as you will be able to access the root causes more easily that way. Then you will ask yourself questions based on whatever you want to understand and change your perception of, you might just want to record the questions on a Dictaphone or phone leaving thinking gaps in between for your answers if you find it hard to remember all the questions, here are some examples:

"I am useless"....Why do I think I am useless?....Why specifically do I think I am useless?....What have I done that is so useless?..... How do I know that I am useless? How specifically do I know that I am useless? Ask yourself the questions until you leave the generalisations (that is vague statements not linked to a specific), until you leave those behind. When you reach the real reason, you can then challenge that reason and see how you have built your story from something very small and feel the weight of your uselessness leave you because you have reached that realisation at a subconscious level, that it has no real basis in fact, you might have to accept that you are not very good at one small thing, but you are not totally useless! If you find yourself saying something like, "everyone thinks I am useless" challenge that with "who specifically thinks I am useless?" We can also follow our challenge to our feelings of uselessness by reversing the question. In what ways have I been useful? In what ways have I specifically been useful? How can I be useful in the future? In what ways can I specifically be useful in the future? Start to build your reverse belief system, your new story. This formula can be applied to all sorts of generalised self-beliefs, but we will just add a few more to get you used to the process.

"I am unlovable"....Why do I think I am unlovable? In what ways specifically am I unlovable? What specifically makes me unlovable? Who has loved me before? When have I been loved before? Challenge that lack of belief in yourself, we all have lovable qualities and we have all been loved at some time by a family member, friend, even a pet, try to find those lovable moments and look at what it is that you are seeming to blame for this idea that you are unlovable.

"Nobody understands me".......What makes me think nobody understands me? What specifically makes me think that nobody understands me? When specifically have I felt that I was not understood? Who does not understand me? How do they show me they do not understand me? What specifically is it that this person does that shows they do not understand me? Conversely, when have I felt understood? Who does understand me? How do they show me they understand me?

Self Appreciation

This is a widely used technique to help you to build your sense of self-worth. I would like you to imagine that you are sitting in a beautiful sitting room...... the colours upon the walls are soothing........ there is a roaring fire in the grate..... you can hear the crackle of the flames..... so relaxing. You are relaxing and reflecting in this room.......you are sitting in a cosy comfortable armchair.......feeling it supporting you..... sinking down into it. You might notice that there are bookshelves upon the walls too..... all your favourite books, your favourite stories, tales of heroes and heroines from the past, from the present and there is a soft carpet upon the floor..........running your toes over the surface, so comforting.........

As you sit there relaxing you remember that you have been asked to write a resume of your best qualities, a profile about you as if you were writing it for someone who did not know anything about you and you are lost in thought, unable to focus. What are your best qualities? Maybe it is hard to write about yourself.

You gaze about the room....... enjoying the comfort there...... when you see that outside the window watching you is someone who loves you. They are looking at you with love in their eyes, they know all that is best about you....... now I wonder if you can imagine floating out of your body from where you sit...... floating out of the window and into the person that loves you and you are looking at you through their eyes. What do they see? What is it they love about you? What would they write in this resume of your best qualities? Focus your mind on their thoughts, seeing yourself through their eyes.

Think of five qualities that they would highlight....... that they would say about you....... as they look at you..... your strengths.... your best qualities. Now float back, back into your body, relaxing in that comfortable room and write down on a piece of paper you had not realised you had been holding,......write down the five words....... or maybe they are sentences, write them down and remember them. Now when you have finished fold up that piece of paper and keep it with you and whenever you need to be reminded of all that you are capable of you can look at it, remind yourself, no false modesty, accepting what is good about you.

Some people struggle with the idea of floating into the image of their loved one, if this is hard for you, just imagine a picture of a loved one looking at you from a photograph on the mantle shelf or on a bookcase, this may be easier to imagine. Also it can be a loved one from any time in your life, it does not need to be current, I have even known someone use an image of their pet who shows them such unconditional love to do this exercise, perhaps not getting specific qualities but a sense of being loved which is just as powerful for building confidence.

Metaphor - Tennis court

There is a tennis court before you......... see the layout of the court .... now a game is in play........ looking at the court....... now look at the ball....... hitting the ball back and forth, back and forth, sometimes at the end of the game....... but before the end of the match the umpire calls for new balls, and the player takes the old balls and hits them hard knocking them out of court....... knocking them out of play........ those doubting thoughts that have been playing around the mind for years...... those thoughts that affect confidence that go back and forth in the mind, it is time to knock them out of play........ off the court....... whenever they pop into the mind, see the tennis court, take the ball, the thought...... throw it high into the air and hit it..... hit it out of the court...... get rid of it.....hit it far away so it is not in play, knocking the doubts out of court and any memories too that have been contributing to that low confidence, using that powerful mind, that creative mind to knock those thoughts far away and begin to use new thoughts..... new ideas.... new ways of being, leaving those old ways behind...... seeing it in your mind clearly.....as the umpire calls for new balls please, in this game that is your life and you can see it in your mind as you take those old balls...... the old thoughts...... and knock them out of play and use the new balls...... the new balls that come your way. Anytime an old memory or thought pops into your mind that affects your confidence see yourself knocking it out of court far........ far away, what a relief now to let it go.

Metaphor - Fairground Mirror for Confidence

I wonder if you have ever visited a fairground, or maybe you have seen one in a film or on TV, in old fashioned fairgrounds they have something called the Hall of Mirrors, the mirrors are concave and convex and they distort your image, you might look tall and thin, or expanded to look fat like a ball, you might look all eyes or all teeth, there are packages on the computer that do it too, I wonder if you have looked at photobooth on an ipad and you can take your image and click on space alien and your forehead expands and you click on bug out and your eyes become bigger, you click on frog and it compresses your lips, I wonder if you have ever done it by accident or design, seen an image of yourself that is all out of shape, I wonder if we can consider....... just consider for a moment that you do not need to visit the fairground or click on a computer to see yourself all out of shape and I am not just talking about body image here....... how you see yourself as a person.......... how you see YOURSELF..... your abilities and your skills....... your place in the world....... I would like to suggest, just put it to you to consider that you see yourself all out of shape, you see the bits you do not like in sharp focus or you blow it up like in bug out....... distorting what is there, seeing it all out of skew......... and that goes as I say for your personality too....... I would just like you to consider how you see yourself........ how you focus on your faults and leave alone all those strengths and abilities so you push your self-image all out of shape......... now what I would like you to do if you find yourself criticising you........... whether you are focusing in on your mind or your body....... just whenever you are taking yourself down....... giving yourself a hard time as you know you do....... I would like you to bring to mind that fairground Hall of Mirrors or that Photobooth and remind yourself, tell yourself that you are putting it all out of shape and that there is another way to see yourself, as other people do..... other people who know you, see you, those who choose to be you partner or your friend........ they see the good bits that is why they are in your life.......... so just reminding yourself through those fairground mirrors that there is a real you out there that is not all pushed out of shape, who has skills and abilities and strengths.......... just leaving that old fairground mirror behind you as you remind you of things undistorted and true. So, from now on whenever you focus in on yourself in this negative way just seeing those mirrors and challenging that image of you....

Affirmations

I am confident and in control, I have all the skills I need in this situation.

I am full to the brim with confidence.

I am confident in all and every situation I encounter.

Depression

About Depression

Depression is a word that is widely used to cover a broad spectrum of mental health issues, from low mood to life situation depression and clinical depression, which can also cover a range of conditions like Bipolar and Borderline Personality Disorder. Before doing any work with self-hypnosis you should be aware of where you are in this spectrum, so it is important to seek medical advice to be sure you are receiving the appropriate treatment, then self-hypnosis can be a useful adjunct to that treatment and assist you in managing your condition. The massive increase in those living with depression is a sign of how our lives are dominated by stresses that we are struggling to manage, our life situations seem to be more prone to change and we are not being taught the strategies that can help us in these situations. We can only gauge the increase based on the number of people being prescribed anti-depressants and at the time of writing this book one in eleven Britons are taking anti-depressants and the increase of prescriptions for anti-depressants is increasing by 20% per year across Europe. It is empowering to find something that you can do to help yourself in a situation which feels essentially out of your control, the first starting point is to realise that you can begin to take some control back from your seemingly overwrought mind.

The symptoms of depression are wide ranging and can vary in intensity, they include, low mood, lack of motivation, low sex drive, poor sleep, repetitive behaviours, low appetite, problems making decisions, self-harm and suicidal thoughts. Some of these symptoms can be specifically targeted and, in some cases, a wider, more embracing approach is needed. At least being aware that there is a problem and you want to do something about it is an important start.

DEPRESSION

Often people want to know the cause of their depression, but this does not always result in a solution to the resulting problems. There are of course many causes and one or a combination of them may be impacting upon you. It can be due to naturally low levels of serotonin in the brain, which can be hereditary, the impact of an illness that enforces life change, or some illnesses like Parkinson's disease actually cause it through low dopamine levels, chemical/hormonal imbalances caused by thyroid malfunction, giving birth or PMT, it can be life situation like bereavement/grief/life changes and alcohol/drug abuse can be contributory factors. This range of causes highlights why it is important to check in with your doctor if you feel the level of depression you are feeling is impacting on your life and well-being.

Depression is in a sense an illness of thoughts and these thoughts will affect us in a literal physiological way. We have already talked about the stress response and how perceived threat can trigger chemicals being released into the body, dwelling on sad thoughts and running those over and over in our heads releases chemicals that reinforce them, but equally, when we think thoughts that make us laugh or feel generally happy, that releases feel good chemicals into the blood stream quite literally making us feel better, we can harness this within self-hypnosis to enable you to switch on the feel good chemicals by yourself, I compare it to changing the channel on the TV, you can select the thought, tune in and begin to feel the good effects. This may sound simplistic, but it is all about shifting our mental focus which we do have the power to do.

Direct Suggestion

Every day I change my mind about things, I change it about whether I want a tea or a coffee, do I turn left or right, which way to go, which way to turn, what can I find now that will help me back on track, making those chemicals in my brain spark it back into life again, using my imagination to create the thoughts that send those endorphins into my mind, or maybe go for a run, lift some weights or swim, I can think about the things that will push my mind into a different place and choose to push it there, taking control again, not free-falling but seeing those chemical levels rise, serotonin increasing, I am making it increase, I have read about the placebo and the nocebo, so which will it be, using the power of my mind to choose the positive thoughts, making those chemicals rise, I can do it, I can, I can...

Indirect Suggestion

Will I notice noticing the changes, to the changes in my mind, that began yesterday, today or tomorrow, as the changes to the changes, will let me know I have found the way.

Metaphor - Retune the Mind

Sometimes the TV needs a retune........ the message pops up on the screen saying on a particular date the channels will be changing, you need to retune the TV or you will lose some channels..... when you click on the familiar number..... there will be nothing there, just a blank screen..... sometimes it might be a favourite channel that is no longer there...... but you may just forget to do the retune and after a while get used to the channels you have, stuck with what you have got even though it might make you low....... to be missing out on something you enjoyed before, but after a while you even forget what it feels like to watch those other channels, watching these programmes day after day, night after night, with no pleasure, no joy, all blotted out....... those old channels now lost in the past..... a past which felt better......... the retune was so long ago now that you have forgotten that it was needed and that there were these other choices out there....... choices that would make you feel better, perhaps you need reminding, perhaps sharing this problem with a friend might let them remind you of that retune...... so you can reset the set and find those lost pleasures, lost stories, ones that made you feel good...... how about starting that retune and finding some of those things you enjoyed before, but do not anymore because they got lost for a while but now they are found, allowing your mind to search and to find........ to search and to find experiences that brought you pleasure........ memories from the past and things lost for a while but always can be re-found, returned, you just have to look...retune the mind, just like you retune that set and receive new channels too, ones you had never found before that can lift you up...........broaden your horizons and free you from that old trap, so much more to choose from now, not stuck in that rut.......... finding your way out again.

Metaphor - Changing patterns - The weaver

I wonder if you can imagine a piece of cloth in front of you...it has a pattern in the weave....it may be many colours.......it may make a picture.....it is made up of different threads.....each individual thread contributing to the pattern woven into the fabric......but is the pattern fixed in the weave? Or if we imagine knitting with wool........ we can use that wool in different colours to weave different patterns into the knitting......we can make it different shapes.....it has the same ingredients ....but it can be a sock or a scarf...a jumper or some gloves...it can have blue swirls....or blue stars....blue stripes.........or crosses....we have the threads to weave and we can weave them as we wish......to make the pattern that we want.......If we do not like the pattern we have created ....we can unpick the knitting.......watch it unravel in front of your eyes...or even the woven fabric can be unpicked....... the threads unravelled and we can start all over again.....we can create a new pattern...... a new garment........ a new shape.....we have all the ingredients we need to reshape it....... to reframe it to how we want it to be...be the weaver of your own patterns.. ...if there is something in your life that does not feel right....unpick the pattern....change it...to one that you want......take control.... take charge....be your own weaver.....take charge of your own destiny.......let go of the belief that the pattern is fixed...that it cannot change.......nothing needs to stay exactly the same....you are the weaver......now weave.........

Metaphor - The Mind – A Screen

Imagine you are visiting your mind for a moment...just a visitor... for a moment.......you see images flashing across a screen....the screen in your mind.....that's what it feels like....watching a story unfold......but is that what it feels like for you?.....sometimes.... just stepping back from those thoughts for a moment....and watching.....watching what happened yesterday.......imagining what might happen tomorrow...rehearsing a conversation... around and around it goes...fragments of speech....words... ideas....all flashing by...stream of consciousness they call it....... and a stream it is indeed........on and on it flows...sometimes it feels as if you cannot keep up with it....you can get swept away with it....with no reality check at all....is this really what I think?....Is this really what I feel? ....Where am I in all this stuff?... these flashing images....dialogues.......ideas.......

But they are all up there in your mind....busy.....busy....busy...all flashing past on the screen...but it is just a screen...so if it is a screen with projections on.......like the old projector at the cinema.......do we have to keep watching........do we have to keep listening.....if we do not like what we see....if we do not like what we hear.....stop.......stop watching that screen......stop listening to the dialogue.....it is time to switch it off....find a different story.....a new film......a better film......one that makes you feel good instead of bad....you are the watcher....the observer......so step back in your mind and decide........what do you want to watch.....you might even hear my voice in your head from time to time....reminding you.......you are the watcher.....watching the thoughts on the screen.......and as a watcher....an observer........ you can choose to stop....do I want to watch this one.............or shall I fast forward to the next......move on......move on to a new story........

Affirmations

I give myself permission to allow myself to release this now, it has served its purpose and I no longer want it anymore.

I give myself permission to change.

I allow myself to see things differently.

Grief

About Grief

Grief is the intense sorrow, sadness and loss caused especially by someone's death, but can be caused by other emotional separations like divorce or family estrangement, it is a feeling of acute emotional pain that is often accompanied by depression. We can also grieve for a possession that is lost, a phase of life, or even for things we have never had like unborn children. There are other issues related to grief such as guilt, not having done enough for the deceased or not having said all that they wanted to say or should have said. We can also have anger with oneself for not having done things differently, like leaving it too late to have a family, or allowing a situation to get out of hand to cause loss, like the repossession of a home. Grief is rarely isolated to one experience of loss, the person who is grieving will relive each loss they have experienced in their lifetime up to that point, if it is a bereavement each death will be re-experienced, if it is a relationship break down, each ending, even with material losses it becomes cumulative and intensifies over time.

Many people have heard of Kubler Ross's work on the five stages of grief, which are: denial, anger, bargaining, depression and acceptance. Anyone who has experienced loss will relate to these, but they are not chronological, you can feel all in one day, veer from acceptance to denial and into anger again, it is a process, and one that has to be worked through, the most intense period of which lasts about two years. The bargaining stage can begin before someone dies or before a relationship ends and carry on for a short while after, as you offer changes to keep the person there, in such situations even people with no faith will find themselves offering a deal to a God they do not believe in. The anger can become directed at the deceased person, the self and anyone involved in the care of the loved one, the anger comes from feeling powerless.

People who are grieving feel a loss of control, death is the great leveller, it cannot be changed, it is all powerful and ultimate, all the bargaining in the world will not change it, thus helping yourself to feel empowered to heal yourself of the pain will be important and finding some level of acceptance. All forms of grief involve this loss of control, if someone decides to leave you it is an ultimate reality you cannot change, as with facing a material loss like the repossession of a home. It is one of those experiences which leads to a transition from one phase of life to another, as when we are young and part of a family unit we feel that everything can be solved by a parent, we feel safe and that they can make everything alright, when we progress into grief we are experiencing that ultimate grown up reality that there are things that no one can fix for us and have to be faced.

Most people experience normal grief, they have a period of sorrow, numbness, guilt and anger. Gradually these feelings ease, and it's possible to accept loss and move forward. For some people, feelings of loss are debilitating and don't improve even after time passes. This is known as complicated grief, sometimes called persistent complex bereavement disorder. In complicated grief, painful emotions are so long lasting and severe that you have trouble accepting the loss and resuming your own life.

In our modern society we do not talk about death, we cannot even say the word, we use euphemisms like "passed away". Particularly in British society we are not meant to show our feelings, it is all about "stiff upper lip" "pull yourself together" People are not, therefore, allowed to engage with their feelings and they have no guidance about how to deal with death. We have lost the old rituals of grief that helped us through the process, we reach an abrupt halt and are expected to just get on with life, which for many is very challenging, especially when the people around you are not comfortable allowing you to speak of your loss or have limited patience to allow you to do so. We protect children from the realities of death, making it even more frightening, because we protect children from things which they need to be afraid of, so when they first have to face it, it is far worse for them.

Self-esteem issues can underlie grief, the griever may have been overly dependent on the deceased, you need to think about the situation of the role of the deceased in your life to fully target all the related issues to empower the recovery. People can romanticise or create a fantasy about the deceased person, they become redefined in death, it is important to find the true story and be honest with yourself about it. You will find a greater honesty with yourself when you tackle some of these issues within trance.

Metaphor - Bereavement - The receiver

There is so much information out there on the internet now....you switch on your computer......your laptop...... tablet or phone and type in what you want ...... the information appears......it is there for you to access to read and to see....... If you want that information and your phone battery is flat or your computer stops working........the information does not disappear....... it is still out there in the ether.......waiting for you to tune in when you can...........you just cannot access it.......it still exists.... somewhere out there.......... you cannot reach it because your receiver is broken or flat.

The same with the TV or the radio,......just receiving a signal,... .....a signal out there in the ether that we just cannot see,.... something we want to tune into........all this information out there on the information super highway ....but we need a machine to access it ....to find it and to see it............. I wonder if your subconscious mind is receiving my message........ my subliminal message that they are not gone......... the receiver is broken that is all...they are out there......you just cannot see them without the receiver.....out there with other things you cannot see with your limited senses…those limited senses of taste …smell……..sight…..taste…..touch and sound……..there are spectrums of light that we are told are there…that we just cannot see…..there are sounds that a dog can hear that are beyond the range of our ears…what else lies beyond the range of our senses….. out there……safe and secure….just on a different channel to you right now……….that's right now allow your subconscious mind to process these words…….take the comfort within………the nugget within that lets you know it is alright……..they are alright and you are too……

Cutting the connection to an old relationship

We are going to use a similar technique here to one we have used for cutting the connection to an addiction but in this case you are cutting the connection to the emotions related to a past relationship, we will start in a similar way as before but there will be some changes.

This process will help to cut your link, your connection to your ex-partner, it does not hurt them at all, but just reduces their impact on you emotionally, even if you are trying to transit to a friendship you will find this useful to shift the perspective on the relationship. It involves a visualisation process within trance that we can compare to a daydream, which we will use therapeutically. First read this process through and then apply the instructions in trance. Use the power of your imagination to see two circles drawn on the ground touching each other like a giant number eight, the circles need to be large enough to see yourself standing in one of them. Now you could imagine these circles painted on tarmac like you might see in a school playground, or painted on grass with white paint, or you might see them drawn in the sand or even as crop circles tramped down in the corn, use your imagination to create these circles.

Now imagine yourself in one of these two circles facing the other circle….. so it is a giant figure of 8 drawn on the ground in some way and you are in one facing the other...... now, in the other circle put your ex-partner or indeed anyone who is having a negative effect on you. Next you will see there is still something that connects you to that person in the other circle........ it could be a piece of thread wrapped around them and then going across the circle and wrapping itself around you........ I wonder if you can see this....... or a piece of rope, a chain, it is wrapped around them and linking it to you...... they cannot enter your circle but they are still affecting you in some way........ what we are going to do now will cut that connection, break it once and for all so they can no longer affect you...... severing that connection so what you need to do now is to look around in your circle for whatever you need to cut that connection, there may be some scissors there, shears, an axe, a knife or even some bolt cutters, whatever it is that you need it is there............ ready for you to use to cut that connection, so now pick up what you have found which will be exactly what you need and cut it, sever it, break that connection to that person now....... see that link, the tie breaks and now you are free to walk away from your circle and you are free from the influence that person had on you...........having broken it at a deep level, deeper than your conscious..... that's right you have done it.......... feel the relief sweeping through you.

You may want to repeat this exercise a few times to really get the impact of it, learning and change comes through repetition, it is how you gained the connection to that person and you are applying similar principles to erase it.

Metaphor - Idealising a past relationship - Rose tinted spectacles

Imagine you are sitting in a comfy chair and looking at an old film that you have dug out about the past....... you in the past...... this past relationship...... now the film begins and you see all the reasons you were together at first..... I know there are reasons that you were together but there are also reasons that you are not together anymore........ so maybe you should stop focusing on the good bits……..what you need to do now is to remove those rose tinted spectacles that you have been viewing this past relationship with………. you need to take them off now, you need to see yourself pulling off those rose tinted spectacles and tearing them away, take them off……..tear them off and throw them away and look at the screen now, you can see the things that went wrong now……….. it is like looking at an image with a magnifying lens and you can see the bits that you have been trying to ignore, perhaps their selfish acts……..or their temper or those things that really got you down, you can remember now the bits that were bad too…….. taking off those rose tinted spectacles and not scooting through edited highlights of the good old days…………. but seeing them for what they were and knowing that you deserve better than this, you need to look for something better than this, now you know that it was not perfect…….. now you can see the cracks and joins that you tried to stick together and ignore.

Now you need to think about the kind of partner you do deserve…..who treats you right, seeing things in a new light, a bright spotlight…… not the soft focusing that hides the blemishes, seeing things as they were and that you can leave this behind now and step into the future……. in fact you do not need to keep this old film you have been playing any more, you can get rid of it, throw it away and build on a new day, a new way……..a new way of seeing things now, no longer viewing the past through these rose tinted spectacles, seeing things clearly now, as they really were……..you deserve something better now……..and the film before you now can maybe see a new person coming into your life, as you have closed the door onto the past, something new is coming into view…..a new beginning now, a new start, seeing that new start beginning now…a new view…a clear new view…that's right.

Direct suggestion bereavement

My grief is s measure of my love, I accept the grief as I accepted the love.

Indirect suggestion grief

I wonder when I will notice my life beginning again.

Direct suggestion relationship breakdown

I need to close the door on this relationship to open the door on the next one, until the last door is firmly closed, I will be unable to step through the next. I am shutting that door now and turning the key.

Indirect suggestion relationship breakdown

I wonder whether it will be in a week, or a month, or maybe three months that I will be ready for that new relationship.

Affirmation

I love and release my loved one.

I let go of the pain and remember the love we shared.

Now is the time to accept.

Insomnia

About Insomnia

We use the word insomnia fairly freely these days, but it is a growing problem, with people more likely to be mentally than physically tired, over-stimulated by artificial light, alcohol and caffeine, whilst being over-run with worry and stress. It can mean a difficulty to attain sleep or staying asleep, many people have long periods of two or three hours awake during the night, some people wake very early and cannot return to sleep. The clinical definition of insomnia requires someone to have difficulty sleeping at least three nights per week and to continue for at least three months and to be having a practical effect of the individual's life situation, i.e. work or school and close personal relationships. Long term insomnia can be a serious problem leading to impaired cognitive function, memory problems, depression and increased risk of heart disease, high blood pressure and impaired immune response.

Bi Modal sleep pattern

One area of insomnia has led to some interesting research, the habit of being awake for a couple of hours during the night, is now being seen as a natural part of the human condition and called bimodal sleeping. It is being argued that in ancient times we would have gone to bed much earlier and then woken for a period during the night and then returned to sleep, more in touch with our primal animal self, as animals rarely sleep for long periods without waking. It is believed that the introduction of gas light and then electric light led people to go to bed later and later and to disrupt the more natural body rhythm for sleep. An experiment has been done depriving people of time inputs in a controlled environment and allowing them to sleep when it felt right for them to do so and they quickly fell into the bimodal sleep pattern. The best thing to do if you are sensitive to your natural body rhythms and are waking in the night, do not lie there waiting to go back to sleep but do something for a short while and then return to bed, then utilise one of the self-hypnosis techniques outlined in this section.

Circadian rhythms

When talking about sleep, we need also to pay attention to the circadian rhythm which is effectively your 24 hour body clock and its functions, which are determined by the body's reaction to light, this is controlled by the hypothalamus, via light sensors in the eye, these detect the light and pass the information on to the pineal gland. When the pineal gland detects the light has reduced, it then produces melatonin, which in simple terms, tells the body it is time to sleep. In the modern world we are deprived of natural daylight, as we spend much time indoors and we use artificial light to extend our natural day, so our circadian rhythms are being knocked out of kilter, in some cases just not having enough light will confuse the balance of this delicate system and some people have a hyper-sensitivity to the alterations of their body clock. It is also important to note that when melatonin production increases serotonin production reduces, which is why things can feel so bleak in the middle of the night if you have a worry on your mind. Serotonin is the feel-good chemical; a certain amount is released during the day and the levels of which are boosted through positive experiences. If someone is not getting enough natural daylight, their brain becomes confused as to when it is supposed to be alert and when to rest as the contrasts are not clear enough. So make sure you get out into real daylight, not muted indoor light and try to keep your exposure to light minimal in the evening leading up to bedtime.

Sleep misperception

There is a condition called sleep misperception, which means that sometimes people feel they have not slept or have had little sleep, when they have indeed had more sleep than they realise at a conscious level. The new technology via monitors that can be worn on the wrist to measure sleep can dispel sleep misperception as people can realise that they have had more sleep than they thought, but this technology can have the reverse effect of exposing how little sleep someone is having, increasing the pressure to try to sleep. This can lead to very obsessive behaviour around sleep.

What can cause insomnia?

There are many different reasons for insomnia that may impact on the best way of dealing with it, such as work patterns: people who have worked shifts that include night shifts for long periods of time will often have problems sleeping, also people who do jobs where they are on call, especially if the work involves responsibilities to act quickly and suddenly like nurses, they will often have difficulty staying asleep. Caring patterns, either caring for children or someone elderly may often lead to a person not allowing themselves to sleep, constantly fearful of not hearing a call for help. Anxiety/worry is obviously one of the biggest causes of insomnia, work or family anxieties that keep going around in the head and the less sleep you have, the less equipped you are to deal with the problems, so it becomes a vicious circle.

Safety can also be a problem, if someone has long term feelings of being unsafe, sometimes people have had experiences that have led them to feel unsafe and it is important to build a feeling of security and safety to cope with the insomnia. Some people have a fear of death and they can make the mistaken comparison of sleep with death deep in the psyche, so keeping awake becomes for them, a way of fending off death. There is a fear of never waking up again. If you have this fear at a conscious level, it is important to remember the number of times you have awoken from sleep, to begin to regain trust that the pattern of waking each day that has established will continue, but we can also look at this at an unconscious level too by doing some work in self-hypnosis.

Alcohol and drug use can disrupt sleep patterns, in fact many people use alcohol to aid sleep, it may get the person to fall asleep, but they often wake a couple of hours later and struggle to return to sleep. Alcohol disrupts NREM and REM sleep (that is in simple terms the non-dream state and the dream state), combined with issues such as dehydration and the need to relieve the bladder will all contribute to the disruption. Anyone suffering an ongoing condition which involves pain, like arthritis, may have trouble sleeping or wake in the night when certain movements trigger an increase of pain. If this is the case for you, it would be useful to use some of the self-hypnosis for pain as well as insomnia.

Many people in old age seem to struggle with sleep, a lack of physical exercise, dwelling in the mind with less outside stimulus, pain issues and the fear of not waking may all contribute to this. Lastly hormone changes can effect sleep, low levels of oestrogen and hot flushes during the menopause will cause insomnia as well as low levels of progesterone at certain points within the menstrual cycle, often a person will have a sleepless night the night before a period, awareness of this can be built into your daily sleep routines.

Sleep Trigger

The subconscious mind is waiting for a trigger to tell it that it is time to take over from the conscious mind. If the mind is whirring or agitated, it will not get the signal and sometimes it can get mixed messages about when it is appropriate to sleep, the brain waves are so active that the subconscious assumes you are not ready for rest. We need to put into the subconscious a trigger that it will recognise as the call to sleep, using a visualisation process that re-enforces the sleep message. I often use the imagery of walking through a forest and sitting under a tree and making the scene as clear as possible, using sights, sounds and even smells to anchor you in the thought and then watch a leaf as it falls from a tree, telling the subconscious that when it sees the leaf falling from the tree, it is time to sleep. If you put yourself into a trance and then do this exercise saying in future it will lead to sleep, then when you go to bed at night work with the same image, your mind should begin to recognise it as a sleep trigger. There are many other sleep triggers you can use, later I will detail a metaphor that combines a sleep trigger and a distraction technique.

Law of Reverse Effect

There is a law of the mind known as "the law of reverse effect", sleep is an area where the law of reverse effect comes into play, it means simply that the harder you try to do something the more difficult it becomes, in this case the more you try to make yourself go to sleep , the more alert you become and sleep becomes even more evasive. Thus, the last thing you want to be doing is thinking about sleep or trying to go to sleep. We can see this law at work in other areas, such as when you are desperately trying hard to remember something like a name for example, it is only when you stop trying so hard, when you remove your focus from the search that you do remember. There are two ways of working with this problem with relation to sleep. Firstly, hard though it may seems, tell yourself to cultivate a mental attitude that sleep really does not matter, saying to yourself that you have gone to work with little or no sleep before, you have survived sleeplessness, indeed some people have been deprived of sleep consistently like in the trenches during the First World War, actually it really does not matter that much so you are just going to lie there and let the night drift past, in fact it is quite pleasant just lying there. Once you have ceased to keep trying to sleep, sleep will come to you. You may have noticed that it is in the morning when there is little of the night left that you fall asleep, this is because you have given up trying, thinking there is not enough time left to sleep.

The second approach is to simply distract the mind to a different topic from sleep, but not one that will be wholly absorbing, this is where the old counting sheep idea came in, using the visual imagery of the sleep trigger may be enough of a distraction. We need to work on the principle that the mind can be rather like that of a child saying "when will we be there" on a long car journey, the best thing to do is distract it by looking at things outside the window, get the mind to do a similar journey, naming shades of colours, birds names, anything that will trick the mind from sleep concerns but as I said not be wholly absorbing.

Strategies to use in conjunction with Self-Hypnosis

Nocturnal routines are important, so having a bedtime routine or ritual helps to prepare the subconscious for sleep, it begins the signalling process that this is what is expected, this is what we do to prepare for sleep, that winding down can begin. In particular subdued lighting as you near bedtime is important and definitely not using a computer or any kind of screen, as the brain responds to the light, telling it that it is daytime and sending the wrong signals, as indeed bright lighting will do. If someone is having chronic problems blue lighting is the one that will create optimum response in the brain for sleep. Avoiding stimulants like caffeine near bedtime or foods with high sugar content is very helpful. Breathing exercises can also help to prepare for sleep as endorphins with relaxing qualities will be released into the blood-stream, so slow deep breaths will help trigger this and be a useful part of a sleep action plan. Mindfulness exercises may also help, such as being mindful in pre-sleep activities such as brushing the teeth, this will help take the mind away from its constant merry-go-round of thoughts and begin to prepare for the winding down process. Bedroom arrangement is also important, the bedroom should be a place of rest and all electrical equipment should be kept out of this space, we pick up on the residual electrical pulses and it hampers the relaxation process of rest. If you must have electrical equipment in the bedroom, make sure it is turned off at the wall. It can be a useful part of sleep preparation to keep a note book by the bed to write down any thoughts that are troubling you, so that it will feel like it has been dealt with and no longer has to go around and around the mind, it can be safely put aside until the morning. It is recommended not to drink anything in the last hour before bed to prevent your bladder disturbing your rest.

Direct suggestion

I no longer need to keep myself awake, I no longer have to work so hard to keep myself awake, I can allow myself to go to sleep now, what a relief that I can allow myself to sleep now.

Indirect suggestion

I do not need to notice the moment that I slip off into sleep and sleep is not something that I do not find easy now. I wonder at what moment I will no longer notice that I am still awake.

I wonder if I will fall asleep the moment my head hits the pillow or whether it will be five minutes after that.

Metaphor for sleep creating a sleep trigger

I can see the seashore, the blue of the sea and the blue of the sky……. the shades of blue, relax me as I watch the sea lap at the shore……. the sea rolling in and out, in and out, like the gentle rhythm of my breath, I wonder if I try………. if I can hear the sound of the sea gently lapping the shore in and out, in and out………. some seaweed lies discarded by the waves upon the shore……. a deep brown like the brown of the earth but glistening there in the bright sunlight, a sunlight I also see glinting off the surface of the sea, the sun high in the sky, warm and comforting………. can I remember a day lying in the sun? how drowsy it makes me feel………. listening to the rhythm of the waves as I drift in and out of awareness, and then there is something floating on the surface of the water………. I wonder why I had not noticed this before………. bobbing gently on the waves…….. that rhythm of the lapping water bringing it closer and closer……….. a green glass bottle………. bobbing on the waves being brought slowly in to the shore….. like it is being called in, pulled in, so slowly but nearer and nearer as I begin to drift deeper and deeper into seeing this scene in my mind as I drift with the warmth of the sun…….the rhythm of the sea and the strain of keeping my eyes open in the light......... watching the bottle coming nearer to the shore....... too much effort now to watch and wait for the bottle to land upon the shore and lie next to the seaweed there, never mind if there is a message there in that bottle......... it can wait until morning......... as when I lie here and imagine this scene it will always take me down into sleep before the bottle has touched the shore...... rocked into sleep by the rhythm of the sea, the heat of the sun and that bobbing bottle out there......... it will be my trigger for sleep, the sign that my mind needs that it is time to sleep........ time to rest and take that journey into sleep and when I awake the bottle will have landed upon the shore......... but I will know it will always take me into sleep as I see it get nearer to the shore as I see this in my mind at night......... my mind knows now that it is time to sleep, that natural rhythm like the rhythm of the sea, the rhythm of my breath and the rhythm of night and day, time to sleep and night.....

Metaphor - The bag

As part of the preparation to sleep routine go into a light trance and imagine you have a large bag in front of you, it could be a large bag like a suitcase or the kind of bag you carry a computer in, or maybe even a handbag, but whatever you choose make sure it is familiar to you so you can imagine it as clearly as you can, if you do not see things clearly just focus on the concept that you have a bag there in front of you and we are going to put into the bag items that symbolise anything that has worried you during the day....... if it is a person, put a photo of them in the bag...... it could be more than one person so put representations of anyone who has troubled you that day...... then symbols of anything else that has bothered you, if it is a work issue....... you might perhaps put something that reminds you of work in that bag, like a computer perhaps, use your imagination to make the appropriate links, for example if you are a driving instructor with a difficult pupil you could put a toy car in the bag to symbolise a difficult lesson.......something that is just weighing you down could be a dumbbell that you are putting aside for the night...... so what you are doing here is finding a symbolic way to put your troubles away for the night so they do not go around and around in your head. So fill your bag with all the things that you want to leave behind for the night and then imagine putting that bag at the side of the bed, now everything is in there so you do not have to take this stuff to bed with you…….. after all you cannot deal with any of these situations whilst you are in bed….. they will be there for you to pick up in the morning if you want to….. but you may even decide after a good night's sleep that you would rather leave them there and just add to the bag before you go to sleep the following night.

Once a week you can imagine emptying the bag and filing away all those pictures and objects to leave the bag empty for the week ahead….. by the time you do this, the strain of the experience will have reduced and they will not affect you anymore.

If it is something important and you do feel you need to deal with it, just take it out of the bag in the morning….. it will feel easier having slept on it, your subconscious will have done some processing for you whilst you slept………. it is far more powerful at resolving things than your conscious mind which is why you need this sleep time to let it do the work for you.

Affirmations

I sleep deep and refreshing sleep.

I welcome deep and peaceful sleep.

Sleep is with me as soon as my head touches the pillow now.

I am sleeping well now.

Pain

About pain

When we are talking about pain here, we mean physical not emotional pain, emotional pain will be dealt with elsewhere. Pain is perceived in the brain as a result of the sensory signals being passed from the point in the body where the problem is located, or in some cases a perceived problem, via nociceptors, these are like detectors that pick up the problem to pass the information on. These nociceptors send signals via nerves to points on the spine, which then allows the brain to find the point of the pain. There are pain transmitting and pain modulating substances which are also released when the pain is detected, this information is passed up to the brain.

Many things are taken into account by the brain when assessing pain, for example, emotional factors can affect how the pain is perceived or 'felt'. As pain is essentially interpreted by the brain, taking in relative factors, it is a relative experience and what for one person can be intolerable pain is quite manageable for another. In experiments it has also been proven now that some people genuinely have a higher pain threshold than others, though why this is seems to be unclear. Certainly, a variety of factors need to be taken into account when measuring and managing pain.

The point of the pain signal is to alert the brain that action needs to be taken to deal with a problem somewhere in the body, thus acute pain can be seen as a warning to the brain, an alert like any protective alarm system. In cases of chronic pain, the nervous system can be more sensitive to new inputs of pain sensation. Sometimes no reason can be found for perceived pain and there are many reported cases of phantom pain in, for example limbs, that have been removed, this makes pain a complex area of study and interpretation, which cannot ignore the psychological 'mind' element in the process. There are a high number of cases of pain with no clear cause reported from people suffering from Post-Traumatic Stress Disorder. It is worth mentioning here that when we use the term PTSD people often think of someone returning from a critical situation like a war, but it can affect people from a wide range of situations when something has happened to someone that feels out of their control like abuse, a burglary, an accident to name but a few. Thinking of the role of the mind in our perception of pain, I wonder if you have ever noticed that if something interesting happens like a phone conversation or watching a good film whilst you have been in pain, your awareness of the pain diminishes as your focus is elsewhere. When treating pain through hypnosis we are working with this ability to distract the mind from the perceived pain and alter the interpretation of the pain signal.

As most pain will have a medical/physical cause, **it can be dangerous to shut off the pain warning signal unless the pain trigger has been properly investigated,** before pursuing any techniques to manage your pain, make sure you have seen a medical practitioner and have a diagnosis for the cause of your pain. Once you have this and are getting the appropriate medical interventions, you can use some of the techniques below to manage and reduce your pain.

It can be useful to keep a pain diary, but only for a short while otherwise the focus on the pain can become obsessive, but a period of observation can highlight factors, such as environmental and emotional factors that may be exacerbating your pain. Ask yourself the following questions:

What is the scale of the pain on a measurement from 1-10 with 10 being the worst?

How well do I feel today on a scale of 1-10 with 10 being the worst?

Do I feel supported by my family or friends today?

Have I eaten healthily today?

Have I exercised today? If so, how much?

Have I done something I enjoy today?

Have I been stressed today?

Use this information to detect patterns that can improve or worsen your pain perceptions and use this to help to manage your pain.

Pain Direct Suggestion 1

Does my pain serve a purpose for me? is it telling me to stop doing something? is it telling me I am tired? is it telling me I am hurt somewhere? I know my pain has a message for me, I am hearing that message now, I am hearing the message the pain has sent me, so that it can stop now, I hear the message of the pain and I am taking it on board, you do not need to shout that loudly at me, pain, I hear the message you are sending me, I am stopping and taking some rest now, here I am pain and I hear it now, so you can turn right off, switch off that message as I have it, I am listening, so you can quieten down now pain, I am giving you some rest now pain, a break from the effort of reminding me again and again, I take it on board, I am resting now pain, so off you go now and leave me to enjoy this peace this relaxing peace, that's right.

Pain Direct Suggestion 2

Whatever purpose my pain had for me, I have found a new way to fulfil that purpose, so I no longer have any purpose for the pain to fulfil for me.

Pain Indirect Suggestion

I do not want you to notice the very moment that the pain has stopped, that exact moment when the pain has stopped, the pain is not needed any more and that you can perhaps stop notice, noticing, if the pain is there or not, that I do not need that signal any more, that signal of pain any more, I do not want you to notice that the moment has passed and the healing is occurring, I do not want you to notice that there is no need for you any more to be aware of pain anymore, you are not needed any more, I got the message ages ago now, so you are wasting your time with me now, I do not need you to notice, noticing that your job is done, because I am better now, my body has done its job, all healed now, healing continuing every moment of the day now and you do not even need to know it is occurring as you switch off now, like switching off the light, job done.

Pain Indirect Suggestion 2

I wonder when I will notice, noticing that the pain has gone, whether it will be right away or whether I will notice in ten minutes or ten minutes more, at exactly what moment will I notice the easing of the pain.

Metaphor – Red Ball

I have found that comfortable position and begun to relax myself…….. finding that quiet place of hypnosis, of trance within and now I am focusing in on the pain…… finding the pain and then seeing the pain as a round shaped ball…….now seeing the pain as a red round ball, now seeing the pain is a red round ball of wax………..yes……seeing that pain as a red round ball of wax, I am seeing it clearly now, clearly in my mind…….. now I just need to find the very centre of the pain, looking for the centre of the pain and when I find it, as I find it, I place a wick in there…….. the wick in there at the centre of the ball of wax and it reaches up and through the top of the pain………. reaching and stretching up through the pain to the surface of the pain and now I am going to light that wick…….. and watch the flame flicker and then the very edges of the pain begin to melt……… the edges of the pain are softening and melting away and the flame flickers….. feeling the edges of the pain melt away and that ball, that red ball of wax is becoming smaller……. watching the wax melt away…… melting away and the pain has eased around the edges as the ball gets smaller and smaller as the candle steadily burns down towards the centre......moving towards the centre of the pain and continuing to melt it away, feeling the pain eases and melting away, the wax cannot withstand the power of the flame as it melts it away....... melting the pain away, feeling it ease, right through to the centre, easing and melting away. What a relief to let it go, what a relief to feel the pain right through to the very centre melting away..........I have control of the pain, I can follow it right through to its centre and dissolve it.......... I can feel the pain ebbing away now, like the ebbing tide, withdrawing and leaving me in peace, a gentle comforting peace, what a relief to let go, to let it go....

Metaphor - Pain control system

My conscious mind does not control my pain....... it is my unconscious that is in charge of my body systems, my heart beat, my unconscious breathing, body temperature, my immune system, my habits, my behaviour, it processes my pain, it deals with transferring all those signals, I guess it is a vast control panel........ a control panel with dials to measure how I feel in my mind, how I feel in my body........ dials relating to every part of my body, from my toes and feet, to my abdomen and hands.......... my whole body.......... all registering their sensations, receiving the signals....... tuning in to the least twitch, ache or stub of the toe........ that pain I am having is registered there.......... on one of those dials, perhaps I could try to see it in my minds-eye...... that control panel there...... zero in to find the dial responsible for registering my pain, seeing that it is turned up high, it must be possible to turn the dial down, I mean people walk across hot coals and lie on a bed of nails......... what are they doing if not turning the pain dial down......... turning down the receiver there, perhaps not switching it off altogether, but turning the dial down to a low level........ just a dull sensation in there........ from high pain to a low dull sensation there..........not a magic trick, just turning down the dial........ the perception in there, taking control of the dial and seeing it twist down, turn down and feel the lightness of sensation there.

Affirmations

I have released the pain now.

I am free from pain, it no longer has a role for me.

I do not need that pain signal any more as the problem has gone.

I am healed so I no longer have pain.

Patience

About Patience

Patience is an increasing problem in the modern world where we have become so used to instant gratification, if we want to buy something, we can have it delivered the next day, we can download books and music instantly, we can watch TV programmes and films on demand. However, there are some things we do have to wait for, a relationship to blossom, news about a job, waiting for a baby to come or the results of an exam. We have lost the ability to occupy our minds and peacefully wait and an understanding of the measure of time will help us understand how we can help ourselves when we are forced to wait. Einstein's theory of relativity shows us that the measure of time, or our perspective of it depends on what we feel about what is happening, when we are having a good time it passes in a flash, when we are having a bad time it feels like it is passing slowly, but time is actually passing at the same rate, it is our perception that changes. With this in mind, we can cultivate patience and an ability to cope with waiting for time to pass, if we occupy our minds fully with something we enjoy, rather than focusing on the object of our intent, the thing we are waiting to happen, as with some other areas of treatment we are looking at distracting the mind, but also developing and understanding that patience is often rewarded.

Direct suggestion

I am patient now, I know how to wait, as I will be rewarded for my patience, in fact I have been rewarded for my patience before, it makes it even more enjoyable when the moment arrives. I wonder if I can remember now a moment when my patience has been rewarded. Waiting for that reward can be a pleasure, enjoying the anticipation of waiting for the reward to come.

PATIENCE

Indirect suggestion

If I have to wait five minutes or ten times five minutes or for one minute less than the minutes I counted before I started to wait the ten minutes, it takes to realise five minutes have passed I will find the moment has come before I can calculate the time as time flies by.

Metaphor – The Kettle

Have you ever sat and watched a kettle boil........it takes just three or so minutes they say, but if you stand and watch that kettle....it seems to take forever to boil........so... so slow as you wait for it to boil......... now if you went away and occupied your mind with other things, that kettle would be done, what about when you are decorating.......... that wall has just been done and you need to paint a second coat........ but if you stand and watch and wait, interminable it will be.......... but occupy yourself in another way and that time will pass so fast, I guess you need to see that time will pass slowly if you watch the hands tick by........ so when you need to speed it up the last thing you need to do is watch......... if you want to get near to any animal grazing in a field, a sheep, a cow, or a horse maybe.......... you need to take it slowly, step by step, that way........it will let you near, so patience will bring to you its own reward.

I wonder when you have been rewarded for your patience..... perhaps learning a new skill........ a language perhaps and then there is that special moment when it all falls into place........ the pieces fit together because you have put the time in........ speaking of putting the pieces together, a jigsaw perhaps......looking at the pieces turning them all over, not pushing and shoving the pieces in, but gently easing them into place, seeing the picture develop and that moment of achievement when it is all in place and the job is done......... I wonder in how many ways you have been rewarded in the past for patience...... just think about it for a while....... let it trickle down into your subconscious and let it remind you of all the times you have been rewarded for patience before.

Performance Enhancement

Improving Performance

Winning begins in the mind. If we believe we will fail at something, the chances are that we will fail, no winning athlete will succeed if they believe there is no hope of success, it is the very moment that doubt creeps in that the ace scorer misses the goal, so you need to believe you can win if it is a sporting activity, or believe you can pass if you are taking an exam. If you have trained either your mind or your body, then you can succeed, whatever anyone else might say to you. The people who achieve success are not put off by failures, but learn from the failure until they get it right. As the great therapist Milton Erickson pointed out, when we are learning to walk we fall down many times until we get it right, until we learn our balance and build our strength, then we succeed at walking, we do not lie on the floor and say it is too tough, that we cannot keep trying, we keep going until we succeed and we can apply this determination to anything we are trying to achieve, to know we will achieve it. Learning takes time, we fall off our bike a few times before being able to cycle then it becomes second nature to us, we believe we can do it, or we would not keep trying. Some of the most successful people were not successful overnight, J K Rowling had her Harry Potter books rejected many times, but she did not give up, she believed in the value of her work until the whole world saw that too. Success comes down to belief and the determination to succeed, so success and winning starts right there in your mind today, winning starts in the mind, so let's use your mind to make you a success, a winner.

Direct Suggestion - Sport

I have trained and worked hard, I am in great shape and now I will achieve my goals, I am a winner at this, I have made the commitment to it, trained my mind and my body and now is my moment.

Direct Suggestion - Exams

I have done the learning that I need, it is all stored in my subconscious mind and when I ask for the information it will be there, the pathway is clear between my conscious and subconscious mind, so I will ask it a question and it will provide me with the answer, because everything that I have ever read and learned is stored away in that filing cabinet that is my mind and all I have to do, is ask, and the information I need will be there for me, so I can relax now and trust that I can pass this exam as I have all the answers filed away in my mind.

Direct Suggestion - Enhancing Memory

When we forget.......the reason we forget....... is often because we have not used our mind with focus......... we have not paid attention.....we have not paid attention to what it is we need to know............ our mind flits from here to there like a butterfly on a summer's day and it misses that thought............the one that it needs.......... its untethered movement......its wild roaming.......... galloping from here to there.....with no direction.....no control...........so the very thing it needs to know............ the very thing it has to remember.......whether it be day-to-day.......... where is my phone? ....Where are my keys?.......... Or something more important.....it just is not there..........we need to take control of the mind...........we need to guide it and direct it to where we want it to go.........then we can freeze-frame it....we can log it and keep it for good........ so what I would like to suggest to you........... when you want to remember..........when you need to remember........ whether it be big or small.......... focus in on it like you are looking at it through a camera lens........ blow up the focus....... see it clearly.......... take a picture of it........zero in on that image and snap............you have it ....save it, file it ....file it in that powerful mind of yours.................you might even want to imagine the filing system in there.......... give that memory a label...... file it and then I think you will find....... when you need it again....... because you have focused in......... copied.......saved it.........it will be there for you next time .....when you need it....it is there.......in fact it was there all the time......but because you had not given it your attention......you had not given it your full attention......you did not know where you had left it....that memory of yours...... I wonder when you will need it again......that specific thought... ....I wonder when you will notice how easy it is to find what you need now.......... because you have given it all of your attention...........it works for sounds too........... the words people say in just the same way............imagine you have a recording device like the one on your phone........... press record and really listen.............really listen to what they say................... then give it a label in your mind.........just as you would on your phone.............. you will find it filed away safely in your mind ....when you need to remember......there it will be .... a way to keep those memories you need close to you........... there when you need them......... all neatly filed away because you have given them your attention............your focus.......... where it needs to be instead of flitting this way and that.......... taking control and honing in on that image........that thought.......... that sound..........and holding it there for a moment......... then filing it away for another day........... that's right.

Positive resource technique for exams

We are going to use anchoring in this technique, if you have not read about how this works look at it in the section on confidence before using this technique.

Visualise an experience you did well, it can be from any time in your life, a time when you felt some kind of special achievement, it could be a time when someone just said well done to you and you felt pride in that fact, allowing your subconscious mind to find for you a moment when you felt you had done something well, or learned something new and it felt good, imagine that and see it as clearly as you can in your mind, if someone else is involved in this memory and they are saying something to you, hear it in your mind, hear their voice, allow all the feelings from this moment to be there. Now put your thumb and finger together and you can feel this feeling of achievement and success, you know you can succeed because you have done it before, channelling that feeling for success and as you step into your exam, place the thumb and finger together and you will feel all the good feelings associated with success and you will know as you sit down to take your exam that you can succeed, you have done it before and you can do it again and you feel all the feelings associated with success to be with you as you sit down to take your exam.

Rehearsal technique for exams

You are ready and prepared for the exams, you have done the work, put in the effort, you know that your subconscious mind has absorbed like a sponge all the information that you have put into it, so now that it is the day of the exam you can see yourself actually relaxed and ready to get on with it, as you have done the work you want to show off your learning, show the examiners just how much you know now. So, seeing yourself relaxed and ready, it is the day of the exam, whether morning or afternoon you feel refreshed, seeing yourself ready and relaxed and heading to wherever this exam will take place and you have used your positive resource, remembered that you have succeeded before and you will succeed again, and if you have experienced any failures in the past, that is where they belong in the past as before you had not worked with your mind in the way you do now, now you know how to harness the full power of your subconscious mind to assist you, you know now all the information is there, filed away for you and all you have to do is remain calm and allow your mind to search for the information for you and send that information to the surface for you, so imagine being ready at the exam and taking yourself through the process of travelling there, arriving there and getting ready to look at the questions whether that be on paper or on a screen, taking your time, there is time for you to read through the questions, they have allowed the time for you to do this and allow your mind to focus on the questions and this moment of looking at the questions is your cue to relax and get on with the work and showcase your learning, allowing your mind to focus in on what is needed, it knows what to do to help you now and at any moment you need to boost your calm and focus just put your thumb and finger together and you will feel that calm confidence moving through you, you might even want to take a deep breath and release those peptides, chemicals into your blood adding to the calm and allowing you to do the work you need to do today, seeing all this in your mind now so that on the day you know exactly what to do, you have had your dress rehearsal, so the real experience goes smoothly and easily for you, working through this in your mind now, in trance now, you know what to do now.

Rehearsal technique for physical performance/sport

Did you know your muscles have a memory, that is how you trained them to walk, that is how you have acquired all the skills that your body has, your ability to hold a pen, your ability to run, to jump, to kick or to hit a ball, your muscles have remembered what they need to do, now I do not know what skill you have developed, the skill you have practiced, what you have taught your muscles to do, but I do know you have worked at it and developed that skill, so I would like you to see yourself doing this sport, this physical activity that you want to excel in, I want you to see yourself as you are when you do it, see the clothing you wear, see yourself clearly, see the kind of footwear you need to do this activity you are going to excel in, know that you have trained your muscles to do what they need to do, to support you with this skill, you have put in the effort, you have trained your body and now your body will reward you and do what it needs to do and your mind is prepared too, you know just what you can do, you know you are a winner, you have trained for this and now you can do what you need to do, your mind and your body are working together to make you a winner, a success, you can do this now, see yourself succeeding in your sport, see the success, feel the moment of it, really work with it in your mind, you achieving what you set out to do, you are a winner, you have done the work, put in the effort and now, now you are rewarded for that effort, see yourself performing just as you want to, see the success and feel yourself succeeding, using the power of your mind and the skill of your body, your body that knows what to do because you have taught it to, your mind and your body supporting you through to achievement, to doing exactly what you want to do, watch yourself in action watch the skill, the ability, it is all there for you now, that's right.

Affirmations

I am a winner! I deserve my success. I have worked hard and now I will achieve my success.

I know I can win.

I know I can pass my exam. I know I have done the work it takes, so now I will succeed.

Phobia

About Phobia

A phobia is a fear or aversion to something, but the fear is significantly disproportionate to the degree of risk involved to the individual, it can therefore appear irrational to the observer who is unaffected by the phobia. In some cases, such as heights, there is a degree of self-preservation involved, but the level of fear displayed is still disproportionate and extreme, to the level of risk that is involved. A phobia is often a conditioned response to a one-off event, or a learning from childhood.

A phobia can create a very physical response as it can stimulate the fight-or-flight response mechanism, thus this internal irrational fear can trigger sweating, shaking, hyper-ventilating, tachycardia, crying and in some cases vomiting and diarrhoea. The activity of this conditioned fear response can be traced to the amygdala part of the brain, as it combines the memory and the fear response to release the hormones associated with the fight-or-flight mechanism.

The phobia may seem irrational to the observer, but it is very real to the person experiencing it and can sometimes have serious consequences. The fear is so deep set that simple rationalising will have no effect. The fear can become so out of proportion that one can reach a point that they would rather die than have to confront or live through the fear situation.

Many phobias are simply programming received from a parent, when we are young this is our only blueprint for life, our understanding about life and appropriate responses and behaviours come from our family. You can find this for example if two children living in houses side by side, in one house the parent screams when they see a spider, thus, as the parent is seen as the person to learn from, they learn a spider is something of which to be afraid, in the house next door the parent calmly puts the spider outside by using a glass and a piece of card, that child learns that there is nothing to fear from a spider. Often in such cases the fear is passed from generation to generation. But what can be learned can be unlearned. The pattern can be changed. Most of us were brought up to believe in Father Christmas, we unlearn that belief in adulthood, yet it was learned as fact, we unlearn or perhaps forget many things we have learned throughout or lives, we learn to stop loving someone who has hurt us for example, so, by looking at your programming in your subconscious mind, you can unlearn your irrational fears too.

Direct suggestion

I learned this fear and I can unlearn it; I know in my conscious mind that there is nothing to fear here, I am now telling my subconscious mind that I am safe and that there is no fear needed here now.

Direct suggestion if learned response

My parent taught me this fear, but I know now that I am not in danger, there are things that my parents taught me that I have kept and are useful to me, but I am not a replica of my parents and some of their beliefs, I have rejected as an adult, this is just one of those beliefs now, so I will reject that too, along with other beliefs I no longer have a use for.

Indirect suggestion

I wonder when I will notice, noticing that the fear has gone, will it be right away, or will it take three days for me to notice or perhaps five?

The Cinema Technique

Visualise yourself walking down the road to a cinema...... see the cinema in your mind, see it as clearly as you can....... now you are outside the cinema..... I wonder what it is called? looking up at the cinema, seeing it as sharp and clear as you can, finding your way towards the door and going inside, if anyone was there when you arrived just allow them to leave, you have the place to yourself...... you notice now that there is no-one else around, the cinema is there for you, for a special presentation just for you. So, you can pick the best seat, your favourite seat.......I wonder where you like to sit in the cinema, finding your favourite seat with a good view and settle down into it, notice how comfortable it feels, noticing the support the seat gives you, so you can really relax down into it.

You are preparing now to watch the film......the film will be about the thing that you fear, but you will be safely watching from the seat in the cinema.......safely watching yourself on the screen..... yourself experiencing what you fear..... but you are not experiencing it, as you are safe in the seat, you will be just watching, anyway it has not started yet....... just letting you know what you will be watching. You are safe and secure and will remain so during this film.

The screen lights up, the feature is about to begin..... you see on the screen an image of yourself, you are watching yourself on the screen and the scenario plays out on the screen in front of you.....watching you, just watching not experiencing....... just observing yourself, like a fly on the wall documentary about the fear...... watching your experience, watching it through and then see the experience you are watching come to a close....... now it has finished......... visualise the image re-winding....... watching all the action going backwards, seeing everything rewinding as you must have seen other films rewind before......rewind....... rewind.........rewind, say this to yourself when you do it in trance, rewind, rewind, rewind, maybe even aware of the sound.......... the dialogue....... any sounds making that silly squeeking sound as the film rewinds to the beginning...... all the action in reverse, watching and listening as it rewinds. Then it stops and all is quiet again.

Now we are going to watch the film again...... having rewound the film to the beginning, let's start again, and you are watching it through again now....... I wonder if it feels a little different the second time, having watched it rewind....... seeing it again, watch it through to the end of the scene you want to work with, watch it play through again and then stop the film. Now we have come to the end, we need to rewind it again......so do that now, see the images all flashing past going backwards this time........ all the action happening in reverse, that squeeking sound as it runs backwards....... right back to the beginning again.

Now I would like you to think about a sound track to this film...... some music which will change the way you feel about it........ maybe a cartoon sound track..... or the theme tune to a comedy you like, or some over-dramatic film score........ just give yourself a moment to think of the sound track for this film, now we are going to watch the film again with this new musical background......watching it through....... now go through the process of watching the film for a third time........ but this time add a sound track........ watching and listening, right through and I wonder if you can notice that you feel different about it now, as the film comes through to the end, just allowing your mind to watch and listen through. I wonder if you will notice that when you are in this situation you have feared before........but do not fear in the same way anymore...... that it feels different and continues to feel different and you may hear the sound track......... the music in your mind and you feel so much easier than before.

You may have found reading this through took you through the process easily, but it may make it stronger to repeat the process quietly in your mind, or record and listen to it giving your mind time to create the images and supply the sounds, rehearsing it through a few times. This will change the way you feel about the fear. The fear will ease and change, the music is a powerful anchor to that change, so think carefully about the music that you choose as it is an important part of changing your relationship to the thing that you fear. This can also be used to take the bad feeling out of any situation that has felt difficult.

Affirmations

There is nothing to fear here, I am safe. My safety is important to me and I know I am safe now.

I have nothing to fear in this situation, I am protected.

I let go of the fear.

I no longer allow the fear to control me.

Physical Conditions

We have already talked about the stress response and the power of the placebo effect. If the body can heal itself by thinking it is taking a tablet which will cure it and if the body can make itself ill if it believes it has been poisoned, we are certain then, that the mind and the body are linked, so what we think effects our body. If getting stressed releases hormones into our body which make the heart go faster and our breathing increase, then again, we are sure that the mind is affecting our body. If this is the case, then we can consider the impact of using the power of self-hypnosis to help manage physical symptoms. In no way am I suggesting this as an alternative to conventional medicine, but as an addition, it can enhance treatments and empower the healing facility in the body. There are a range of suggestibility tests that highlight that mind-body-connection and we have examined some of the more simple ones, such as imagining the sharp taste of lemon juice and the infectious nature of a yawn, how wonderful then to access this mind-body-link and harness it for our own benefit. We have over the centuries moved further and further away from the awareness of this link between what we think and what the body experiences, we have tried to divorce them, this does not help us in any way towards a healthy future, we need now to become aware of that link again and to use it for our highest benefit.

IBS (Irritable Bowel Syndrome)

IBS is a problem which effects the gastrointestinal tract, leading to symptoms of cramping pain, constipation and diarrhoea. Food is moved through the digestive system by muscles expanding and contracting, this enables the food to pass through, however people who suffer from IBS experience problems with these muscles, which can be contracting too quickly, too slowly or just in an irregular pattern. If the food passes too quickly, not enough water is absorbed and this will create symptoms of diarrhoea, if the process is too slow the result will be constipation as there is not enough water left in the passing food, which later in the process, once all the nutrients are absorbed, becomes waste. There are many theories surrounding IBS, but in most cases, there is a stress trigger that exacerbates the condition. The initial problem can be caused by a bacterial infection, an imbalance of bacteria in the gut and possibly issues concerning the messaging between the brain and the gastrointestinal tract. People who suffer from IBS often live in fear of an attack at an unsuitable moment and so they become overly focused on the functions of their digestion, such as what they eat, when they go to the toilet, some even fearing to leave the house if they have not had a bowel motion that morning, thus it can be very disruptive to a normal lifestyle. One of the most important aspects to overcoming IBS is relaxation, in all studies of treatment of IBS, this has been shown to ease symptoms, so any self-hypnosis work you do should provide some support even if you do not use specific IBS related scripts.

Metaphor – IBS – Trains

I wonder if you have waited at the station for a train to arrive...... I find it is best not to stand around and look at your watch, pacing around....... but to become absorbed in something else you could look at your phone and send a message to a friend or check out what is happening on Instagram or Facebook .....read a book or a magazine.......look around and observe what other people are doing and I wonder if you have ever noticed if you are absorbed in this way...... that is the moment when the train will come, because you are not looking, not waiting.....but absorbed in another way....... you could start an interesting conversation with someone at the station as you wait for that train and sometimes there are delays due to leaves on the line and they send a special train through to clear the way. Whatever your journey entails......... watching your watch and pacing around will not make that journey happen more quickly............ or even slow it down.

IBS direct physical

As you relax there I want you to think about the complex machine that is your body, that takes in nutrition and processes it and passes out the waste, it is an incredible piece of engineering and every single cell needs to play its part in the process, we need to think about the fuel we take on board, the right nutrients for us and I am sure you do not need me to tell you what to eat or when to eat, when to eat a large meal, not late at night of course, you know all about that, you know about eating the right foods and which are the foods that are not helpful to you, I wonder if you can imagine your body working through the processing of that carefully chosen food and drink, imagine how each part needs to fulfil its purpose, perhaps for a while there has been a fault in the system, but we are correcting that now, the wrong messages had got through, the messages that made it all too fast or far too slow, because your brain needs to tell your digestive system what to do, give it the right instructions, you can make sure the right messages get through, the gentle rhythm of your inner body, the muscles creating the gentle steady rhythm that moves the food through your system, carrying it along through the small intestine into the large, absorbing just the right amount of fluid, moving steadily along, a steady pulse of digestion like the steady pulse of your heart, the in and out of the breath, the expansion and contraction of the muscles that take the food along, not too fast, not too slow, that's right, you can tell your body what to do, to follow that steady rhythmic pace, taking the food on its journey, taking the nutrients that it needs, until all that is left is the waste products, which you can release and let go of, all at a steady pace, a gentle pace, not too fast, not too slow, following the natural flow of your body.

You can take control as you stay so relaxed now, when we stay relaxed the body understands what to do, if we move into fight or flight response the blood flow gets diverted from that digestive system, leaving it unsupported, unable to process the food easily, unable to carry it along, it either gets rid of it quickly, passing it on too fast so you do not get the nutrients you need or it stops, comes to a halt, a freeze in the process, halting all until the storm is passed, the crisis is passed, so keeping relaxed and calm, choosing calming and relaxing thoughts actually helps your body, your body to do what it needs to do, to get the nourishment it needs and let the rest pass through, so what are you going to do now, will you help your body now, seeing it working smoothly and easily, all flowing through, like the steady flow of a river, or maybe the canals of old, taking their goods from one place to another, a steady flow that canal, just waiting at the lock for the right moment and then on it goes, as you wait at the lock and then it is the time to go, letting go, no pain or discomfort now because you have controlled the flow.

Indirect suggestion for IBS

I wonder when I will notice, noticing I have not been thinking about my IBS all day.

I wonder when I will notice feeling free to go wherever I want because I am not worrying about my digestion any more.

Hot Flushes

Hot flushes affect many women during the changes in hormone levels during the menopause, it seems to be due to the changes in the delicate balance of the hormones with each other that affects the body's thermostat. It is a physiological fact, however women in the menopause can be particularly suggestible, just the mention of a hot flush can bring one on, so we need to harness this suggestibility to also switch it off. Being around other women with the menopause can create a chain of flushing from one to another, so working with mind body control can be very important, not just in stopping a flush, but preventing it starting in the first place. Using one of the following techniques can prevent one starting if someone near you is having one, or if you are in an environment that you know is likely to trigger one.

Metaphor - Hot Flushes - Cold bath

Imagine turning on the cold tap and running a deep bath..... see the bath in front of you, the shape of it, the depth of it, the colour of it and see the cold water splashing into the bath and filling it up....... now I know you feel warm at the moment, but I want you to imagine putting one foot into that cold bath and immersing it....... feeling the cold sensation spreading up your leg..........now put the other foot in and feel that cold spreading up the other leg, now slowly lower yourself into the bath......... the cold might be a bit of a shock at first, feeling the cold spread up your body as you lower yourself into the water........ now lie right back into the water so it is hovering around your neck...... now remember you are not watching this you are experiencing it....... feeling the cold water lapping around your body, surrounding your body, feel the coolness, lying back in the water and feeling the pleasure of cooling down..... if you start to feel too cold....... you can get out of the water and towel yourself down and then wrap yourself into a towel and feel that your body temperature is now just right....... not too hot and not too cold and you can do this exercise any time you want to, wherever you are....... just close your eyes for a moment and allow yourself to remember the cold water feeling....... sweeping through you........ whenever it is safe to close your eyes just for a moment you can cool yourself right down.

If you want to make this a very powerful experience for yourself, take some time to actually get into an ice-cold bath, really experiencing the sensations and holding them as your absolute focus, fixing them in your memory, which will make it easy for you to reproduce the sensations when you want to. You might find you want to use your own words afterwards to describe how that feeling of cold was for you, to assist your mind in recreating it for you.

Metaphor – Hot Flushes – Thermostat

If you have any kind of central heating, you will be familiar with the thermostat, if it starts to get too warm in your home you just get up and go over to the thermostat and turn it down, I wonder if you can imagine doing that now, or if you do not have a thermostat, check out how someone else does it or even google it, it is quite simple, a dial with numbers on, see it now......we have just the same controls for our body....... we have just lost the awareness, the familiarity with which to use it, we take it for granted that our body and our mind know what to do, but during the menopause that all changes...... the fluctuations of our hormones send the thermostat off kilter.....it is running out of control..... we need to get that control back and just as we can have conscious and unconscious breathing we can take control of that thermostat, see it in your mind as a dial........ like you have just imagined but this is inside your mind, the controls you have now, just imagine turning the dial down, you have the ability to do this now, to take control now...... focus your mind on that inner dial and right now, turn it down and you will find as you regain control..... getting the control back as you relax your mind and get into your subconscious you can take control and cool right down, what a relief to know you can take control back and cool right down now, turning that dial up and down as you need to when you want to, that's right.

Direct suggestion

I can tell my body what I want it to do and I am telling it now to cool down, I am cooling down, my body cools down now.

Indirect suggestion

I wonder how soon I will cool-down, will it be right away or in a minute's time or maybe two.

Immune system

Your immune system is there to protect you from infection by bacteria, viruses and parasites. It is not controlled by your conscious mind, but the subconscious keeps it vigilant, on guard and on the look-out for trouble. It will detect anything abnormal, anything it does not recognise as part of your body systems as an invader and then sets about neutralising it, so that it cannot do any damage. If you have had the same infection before, it will be quicker to detect it and control it, as it keeps a memory of all unknown substances, a bit like a security system with face recognition. There are primary and secondary elements to the immune system, if the first attack on the invading organism fails, a stronger force is brought into play. It can be helpful if you have been exposed to an infection or if you are fighting an infection, to give it a boost in trance, to remind the subconscious mind to keep the immune system on the look out and do its job, like giving a motivational talk to some workers, reminding them of what they need to do and indeed how much you rely upon them to do it. We can do this through metaphor or with some more direct instruction.

Metaphor - Immune System – Security

Imagine a large four-sided house, it is on a grand scale like a country house, it has entrances at the front, the sides and the rear. See this house clearly in front of you now, it can be as you want it, look as you want it, because it is your house. At each of the entrances there is a security man or woman, they will check the ID of every person who wants to enter this house, it is a special house, it needs to be kept safe, so they are being very careful with security, no one gets in without identifying themselves, they are keeping this house very secure, even the windows are alarmed so that no one can get in without being checked. Now I would like you to imagine that one of the guards at one of the doors has fallen asleep for a moment……. no one has tried to enter their door for a while so they just nodded off for a second, in that second someone just slipped in without showing their ID…….. but a detector just inside the door goes off and lets security know that someone unknown is in the building and the team gather……. following security cameras to find the intruder and they escort him off the premises, now sometimes someone tries to slip through a window, because there is something of great value in there…….. but the security system quickly picks up the intruder and again………. successfully the security find the intruder and escort them out, sometimes the same person will try to get in again and again....... but the security is there to protect the building, protecting the precious person inside............ and I am sure you are aware this is a metaphor for how your immune system works, constantly on guard, on the look-out for trouble...........virus or bacteria try to get in but the security of your immune system is constantly on guard to protect you, but if you feel you have been around an infection, or you feel poorly for a while.........just imagine doubling that guard, send the security on the hunt and send anything unwanted packing, you could even see it being searched for and found and pushed out the door.......... you can increase your vigilance, ask your immune system to increase its efforts, increase the security to keep you safe......... safe and secure now, no one will beat your immune system............. it is experienced and knows what to do, so even if a virus or bacteria slips in when it is caught napping, it will be hunted down and expelled. You are safe and secure and well, strong and healthy as your immune system does its work for you, taking care of you now, that's right.

Direct Suggestions

My immune system is powerful and it protects me, I have nothing to fear, I can heal myself.

I do not have to work hard to stay well now as I know my immune system is there to take care of me and it cares for me well now, as I become more and more well, well I am and well I will be as I am taking care of me now.

Anorgasmia/difficulty with orgasms

Anorgasmia is a problem reaching sexual climax and involves a combination of physical, psychological and emotional factors, it is rarely a physical problem alone, though some medications can interfere with sexual function. It is often a problem that starts in the mind, a fear of letting go, a result of experiences of abuse, or a child being given a feeling that sex is something dirty and not allowed. So, work on this will involve creating a feeling of safety and a belief that sex is a natural human response and giving permission to the self to enjoy it.

Metaphor – Anorgasmia - The Waves

You are a part of nature........ like the waves that crash upon the shore........ or the air that stirs in the breeze or the cat that curls up on the mat....... we are not apart from it....... but we belong to it, imagine that wave, the surging tide, I wonder where it begins, some way out from the shore a small gathering of force......... a building of pressure which builds and it builds and you can see it coming as you watch on the beach........ you can see the water rising and see its strength build and you can see the crest of the wave as it reaches its highest point........... see it now in your mind as that wave reaches its peak and then down it comes as it crashes onto the beach........ an incredible release from the build-up of that tension and forward it rolls, reaching out along the beach, unfurling, the pressure abated, the force of nature released, as the white foam spreads up the beach and then withdraws into itself again, no one says the tide is unnatural as it ebbs and it flows...... or the rabbits and the cows as they do their thing, nuzzling and rubbing........we accept it is natural, just what they do, after all without it none of us would be here, so allowing that feeling to come as you are part of nature too, like the tide you can allow the passion to rise within........ no-one would try to hold back the tide....... so, allowing your tide to flow, the passion to flow, giving yourself permission to let it go and ride the wave of passion....... like the surfer on the beach, the wave is part of nature and you are with it too, going with the flow, like the birds and the bees, allowing and giving and letting go.........just so you know, how it is to allow yourself to feel the passion within, perhaps seeing that wave building and reaching its highest point and then letting go....... it is not unnatural to want to love and to feel, allowing now, permitting now, knowing now that you are allowed to go with the flow, the flow of the passion within, giving yourself the pleasure that comes from deep within, passion building, no need for over-thinking............your body knows what it needs to do........ so not getting in the way with unnecessary thoughts, just going with the feeling, touch, sensation, that is all that matters right now, leaving thought behind......... and sensing and allowing and enjoying that orgasmic flow........ that's right.

Direct Suggestion one

You are allowed to feel passion as it is a natural urge, a natural need like the need for food, the need for a drink, you are part of the natural world and it is natural to want sex, it is natural to enjoy sex, if you learned it was something bad, you can unlearn this now, just as you unlearned other things in the past that you no longer believe in or even remember and your subconscious mind knows how to do this for you now as we give it the instruction to unlearn for you anything that has held you back from enjoying sex now.

Direct Suggestion two

I am so immersed in my body sensations and thoughts are suspended, I do not need to notice, noticing the moment that I come, whether it will take five minutes or maybe ten, the minutes do not matter in my mind, I may wonder whether it will be now or in a minute or two but I do not need to wonder about the wondering my mind will do as I slip in and out of my body awareness and just allow it to do what it can do for me to find the pleasure I seek, like a game of hide and seek, suddenly it will be there and I will find what I seek, though it has hidden from me before it does not hide from me anymore.

Affirmation

I give myself permission to enjoy sex to the full now.

I allow myself to feel aroused and let go of my orgasm to release it and allow it to be.

Skin Complaints

Many common skin complaints are perceived to have a psychological trigger, at the very least it is acknowledged that stress can play a big part in stimulating skin conditions. So much so that there is now a medical discipline called psycho-dermatology. If you have a skin condition it may be worth examining when the condition began and if any significant life events may have been happening at the time, such as a major bereavement, relationship breakdown or other major life event. It does not need to be a negative event that can trigger a skin reaction, a positive one like getting married, where there is an increased pressure or focus of attention can have an impact on that mind-body-connection. We need to remember that the skin is the largest organ of the body and if we accept the premise of the mind-body connection, then there is plenty of scope for any emotional or psychological problem to be reflected in the skin.

We know that stress has an impact on immune health too, which can be reflected in the skin, our first barrier to infection, it is believed that the stress response can release inflammatory molecules into the skin, which can lead to itching and eczema. Anyone who is sceptical about that link between what we think and our skin, only has to remember a moment of embarrassment and how the skin can flush to realise the strong connection there. There is a whole wealth now of academic research in this area and a high percentage of success for an induced state of relaxation and positive suggestion. You can try a method linked directly to stress, as well as something targeting the skin more directly.

Metaphor – Skin Complaint - The waterfall

Imagine walking through some woods..... see the trees around you..... aware of the green of the leaves fluttering on the trees....... perhaps aware of that familiar fluttering sound of the leaves as a breeze blows through the branches..... maybe there is sunlight, just peeping through the branches as they sway gently........ you can hear the sound of water in the distance, but it becomes louder as you walk, you may notice the sound of a twig snap beneath your tread, walking on...... noticing a damp smell from the wet earth, as you carry on walking noticing the brown of the bark on the trees, maybe some ferns nestled at the base of some of the trees........ or even some mushrooms scattered across the woodland floor, on you walk until you step out into a sunlit clearing and see before you a huge waterfall, the water cascading down in great torrents....... it is such a warm day, you have become so warm from your walk, that you feel compelled to step into the pool created by the falling water and wade out under the waterfall...... it pours all over you......... you feel the coolness of the water covering your skin soothing like a balm........ as if it had some chemical compound in there that takes away all sensation in the skin...... anaesthetising....... alleviating all sensation there as you feel the water........... pouring over you, turning your face up into the water and feeling that wonderful cooling soothing sensation pass right through you..........you can do this whenever you want to and you feel your whole system cleansing, relaxing, tension easing and sensations altering as the coolness changes that sensations, allowing that feeling to sweep through you....... wash through you, ease through you, that's right.

Direct Suggestion

That sensation in my skin was there to alert me to the problem, I understand that and am grateful for being alerted to the problem, but now I know about the problem, my skin can clear up now, I have received its message and it can heal now. I can allow my skin to heal now, message received and understood, I will deal with the problem now, I will take it from here, the part of me that created the skin issue to alert me can go off duty now and allow the healing to occur.

Nausea

Nausea is that awful feeling that you are going to be sick but does not always mean you will be sick. There can be many reasons for it, such as an infection of the gastro-intestinal tract or any of many viruses and bacterial infections. Problems with balance and the inner ear can cause nausea, as can hormonal changes in pregnancy and during periods. Nausea is also often associated with fear and stress, as the stress response when acute will be trying to get the body to rid itself of any extra ballast, that would hamper the body if it needed to run, hence vomiting and diarrhoea when nervous, often though just the feeling of sickness is there and it does not progress to actual vomiting. Whatever the cause, the technique to combat it is similar to pain, it is utilising distracting techniques, there is one below, but there are other scripts in this book that can be adapted such as in the pain section and the anxiety section of this book.

Metaphor – Nausea – Distraction

I know you are right now focusing on your head, because the nausea sensation is located there..... perhaps some pain too...... you are aware of the nausea locked in your head.......so you can leave it there and go elsewhere.....perhaps following your attention from your stomach down your legs........there is no sickness there............no sickness in your legs......so why linger in your head when you can go to your legs...a place where there is no sickness....or now, right down your leg.....your right leg.....into your right foot.....taking your awareness to your right foot....or if you prefer it can be your left....left and right....right and left..... into the foot....aware of the foot and the toes there...examining each in your mind in detail...the foot...the toes...five toes and then it is ten, all those toes, is there a sock or a shoe....head to toe....taking yourself to the toes and letting that sickness go....you can choose to feed it....focus upon it and wallow in it, or lock it away and go somewhere else...somewhere with no discomfort... such a relief to leave the awareness of that locked up there and you go down here...drifting down to your toes...and you can do this any time you get that feeling....to avoid that feeling you do not want and focus all your energy and awareness down there...

right down there.....or left down there....down in your toes....
that's right....each toe in turn from the smallest one to the biggest
one, on the left and on the right....choosing your focus....sending
that mind to a different place.....down from the face right into the
toes, via those legs left and right....

Trust your body

Your body knows how to take care of itself....your body works
around the clock.....tick tock around the clock.....your heart
rate.......pumping supplies around your body......your breaths in
and out....whilst you sleep......and whilst awake that steady
rhythm........natures has its rhythms...the rhythm of the sea as it
rolls in and out.....predictably......reliably in and out.....in and
out.......one of nature's laws.......like the planet turning......the
moon rising and falling..........predictably.......reliably ......your
body is part of that natural cycle.........the sun rising and
falling.........that's right........there is no reason for it to let you
down.......safe and secure.......following nature's rhythm.......
trusting your body....has it ever let you down......those thousands
and thousands of breaths.......the steady rhythm ....your steady
rhythm......always there........like the moon and the sun......
rising and falling.....thousands upon thousands of times.......
that's right........trusting your body.....those unconscious
breaths......up and down......in and out.......we do not even have
to think about it.....it just gets on with the job.....taking care of
you now......allowing it to get on with its job.....not getting in the
way........just letting it do what it needs to do.....that's right..........

Affirmations

I am well and strong.

My mind is in control of my body now, I can heal.

Nature is good at healing and I am nature.

Resilience

What is resilience?

Resilience is something we all have, but in varying degrees, it helps us to adapt to situations, cope with life changes, whether they be work stresses, health issues, relationship problems or family traumas, some people have the capacity to recover more quickly than others as they have greater resilience. This has become the buzz word of the moment with the focus on helping people to build their resilience. Having a strong sense of self, a sense of personal well-being and security will contribute to your levels of resilience along with having suitable coping strategies. It is something that is affected by your life experience, but it can also be developed, and we will look at ways of doing this.

People with low confidence levels tend to have more limited resilience, but it is a life skill, a life skill that can be learned and if learned can impact on confidence levels, if a person sees themselves coping with life pressures better, it raises self-esteem, so it has broader benefits than simply coping better with stressful life situations.

Resilience starts with that perception of who you really are at a deep level, this is sometimes referred to as the core self. We are born into this world unaffected by others' judgements and behaviours, we have an essential self that gradually becomes affected by the environment we grow up in and our early life experiences. Let's look at some of the early factors that might affect your resilience levels:

We can learn from the family we grow up in to feel secure or to feel unsafe; If we grow up in a loving family then we have a sense of belonging, or if not a sense of rejection, of feeling not good enough; If you have the experience of parents battling for financial security and never having enough money, you will grow up with a fear of financial insecurity; If your parents praise you a lot growing up, it will give you a stronger sense of self-worth and entitlement, if you are constantly criticised it will affect your levels of self-esteem and leave you battling for recognition and love; bullying at school is a big factor in eroding the sense of self, as children can be very cruel and being on the receiving end of bullying, taunts and name calling can stay deeply embedded in the psyche affecting behaviour for life if not tackled; a strong friendship base in childhood and indeed in adulthood will impact on overall well-being and resilience, as loneliness and isolation lead to overthinking and feelings of being disliked or unloved.

Obviously, as we grow there are basic needs that need to be fulfilled at a practical level like shelter and food, then after this we have emotional needs that will be met at varying degrees, then beyond that we learn about how to care for ourselves, how to deal with people outside our family units, how to think for ourselves and solve problems that might arise. If the essential core self we have been talking about feels safe and has its emotional needs met and learns how to take care of itself, it will be more resilient. It also needs to have a clear basis in reality to be able to make what we call a reality check in various situations to keep the self anchored in reality. We looked at this in our section on confidence.

With all this in place, life can throw events at you such as bereavements, relationship problems and financial hardships like redundancy that will challenge you at fundamental level, but resilience that has been long established will affect how these situations are managed and make recovery manageable and indeed possible.

Someone with low confidence levels and low levels of resilience has usually been affected by many of the issues we have listed, like not feeling that basic security in early life or being bullied for not fitting in, struggling to make those social connections. It can become a chicken and egg situation, the lack of confidence blocks access to things that could improve resilience, the lack of resilience impacts on the low confidence and it becomes a vicious cycle. If we can work on the confidence and begin to compensate for some of those missing basics, then we can build individual resilience which will, in turn, boost self-esteem, knowing you can cope in a situation that is challenging is hugely empowering. We have already looked at the confidence building elements, but here we will look at an exercise to work with resilience by focusing on positive life experiences which we will often overlook.

Story Telling

This is a technique that boosts confidence, develops an individual's resilience and can assist with all sorts of other life difficulties. Firstly, you need to gather a lot of information about your life focusing on events that have felt like an achievement, or something you can be proud to have done. This needs to reflect all aspects of your life, to take in a whole life, so it could be the moment you learned to swim, passing a driving test, getting into college, standing up to someone, supporting a friend, doing a small gesture of kindness that made a difference, surviving a traumatic relationship breakdown, bringing up your kids, taking an unusual holiday that took you outside your comfort zone, it can be a whole range of types of things that you have experienced, but keeping focused on the positive. It can seem like a huge challenge at first, so I recommend you get a good friend to help you with this, get them to talk to you and draw you out in conversation about your life's better points and get them to take notes. Just the process of gathering this information is therapeutic in itself, as you are being encouraged to find positivity which may often be veiled behind the current issues with which you are struggling.

Once you have this information gathered, you need to collate it and turn it into a story which you will tell in the third person. It maybe you want to write the story chronologically, or to focus on particular character traits. Open the story with: I want to tell you a story of a woman/man I know, then begin your story, if working with a character trait you could for example say, she has incredible courage, you know she had this experience.... and she also did.... such an example of courage this woman I know. When you are moving into a new part of the story you can break it up with expressions like: did I mention he/she............when I was telling you that story of the man I know I may have forgotten to mention how he......When writing up your script pay attention to the rhythm and the rhyme of the language, it helps the story unfold and it carries the listener along blocking out any resistance that you may have.

Even though when you begin the fact finding it can be hard, with someone else's help, it is truly amazing the stories that come out, your friend will no doubt find hidden stories about you they had no idea about and that you had played down or lost sight of in the mists of time. It is amazing how so many people have a distorted view of themselves focusing only on the negatives and playing down their achievements, it is an indictment of our society that people feel unable to acknowledge what they are good at and play it down in a self-depreciating way, whereas if it were someone else they would admire them for what they had done. The process of writing this as if you were writing about someone else is part of the therapy as you will begin to see yourself more objectively, more clearly.

This is one of the exercises you will have to record onto a Dictaphone, computer or phone, record a relaxing induction and then recount the story you have written about your life, but it must be in the third person, not in the personal "I" this stops you resisting direct praise or bringing in false modesty, it can get you to really connect with your achievements, you would not play down someone else's achievements, it gives you a whole new perspective of yourself.

When you have finished the story, tie it in with something you are working on, such as confidence in a particular situation. You can say, clearly this woman/man I know has achieved such incredible things, standing in front of that audience is not going to be a problem for this woman I know, or giving up smoking will be easy for this woman I know, she has coped with much bigger things.

Whatever you use this technique for, it will boost resilience as it gives you a perspective on the self.

There are two examples here to introduce you to the writing style:

Example Story telling one

I want to tell you a story about a woman I know, she has the most incredible resilience, she was really enjoying her job, doing really well, running a charity in London and then she became ill, she was not worried, at first it felt like the flu, but after a while she got worse and worse, she nearly died, now she came through that, and thought that was the worst it could be when she found as she tried to pick up a book when she was recovering, she could not see to read it or write not at all and when she got out of bed she was so weak and slow and she wondered how she would manage, how her life would be? she could not cook a meal or even pick her clothes, even when she was told she would never read and write again as she had damage in her brain, she did not give up, she was not prepared to just give in, so she retrained in a new job which would not need her sight in the same way and did all her learning through listening and it was so challenging at times, but this woman I know would just not give in and she carved a whole new life for herself and do you know what, over time, very slowly over time she began to see again, not like it was before, but it was a chance, just a chance to get her life back again, I guess when I think about this woman I know, it is this part of her story that comes to mind but there is more, so much more to tell you..

Now I could mention, how when she was a teenager she had panic attacks, it all started with watching a disturbing film, from then on, any strain and the panic attack would come back again, but although it worried her she would not take the Valium the doctor gave her and kept on going with her studies and one amazing day she was offered a fabulous job, a job at a newspaper, now this felt way out of her league, but she met the challenge head on and she got promoted in a year and a year on, yet again, until one day she sat there with 21 staff around her and thought how did I get here, I was so scared and worried and now I am the boss and she wondered if she knew what to do and she did, you know, she did really well and she loved it and found within her a competitive streak and a drive that had been covered in those teenage years and one day she sat in a chauffeur driven roller and wondered where that shy girl had gone, who had panic attacks whenever she had to talk to someone new and now she did it every day and even told people what to do, how exciting it was for this woman I know to break free from her fears and live the life of her dreams. Of course, that was all before that illness that nearly took her right down, but she is a fighter she is this woman I know.

Strange as it may sound if you asked her what her biggest achievement was, she might say passing her driving test as it was during those stressy, scary days that she took up that challenge and she kept telling herself she was not very good, but her driving instructor said it was just that nervous thing of hers and she would be really good if she just chilled out for a while, she was so surprised when her examiner said she had passed her test, she said "are you sure?" and he said why?, what should I have failed you on? "Oh, nothing" she said clutching her piece of paper and scuttling away in case he changed his mind, she just could not believe she had done it, but she did, as always, she met the challenge in those early days too…a grim determination, pressing on…….

I guess in this story I am making her sound very serious, but when I think about this woman I know, I think about how she loves to laugh and how she likes to tell a funny story, captivating her audiences and perhaps stretching the truth a little if it will get a bigger laugh. It all started when she was a little girl and she would sit in front of the mirror and practice her impressions of famous people and take any opportunity to practice on the adults around, there was this one time on a long car journey, she was in the back of the car with two family friends and she had them laughing so much that her father who was driving threatened to stop the car as he could not concentrate, due to all the laughter back there and this is a story, a story still told by those family friends of this woman I know. Now along with the entertainer, is the nurturer somewhere in there, as she loves to cook, there is nothing she loves more than inviting guests for dinner and will be thinking about the menu weeks in advance wondering what would suit people best and taking care with the ingredients and loving the providing and the caring and hoping there will be enough for the guests to take home and she even delights in preparing the table so it looks inviting for her, that is just how she is this woman I know.

She loves learning something new, a new language, a new skill, just keeping that lively mind going, providing new fodder, new material for it to turn around and around, I guess she has learned from long ago to divert that active part of her mind that as a teenager told her there was something to worry about, to divert this part of her mind into new learning and new thinking and occupying it in this way and it gives her great joy and even when she could not see, it did not stop her, she would be there, with her reading machine turning the pages and following through with new knowledge and ideas to go over in her mind.

She is a healer now, one of those new learnings I was telling you about, a healer she is this woman I know and who knows how many people are so much better for the work she has done and I sometimes wonder if it was these challenges she has met, that make her find it easy to understand the troubles of others, the battles to survive and she opens the door to them to new ways of thinking, new ways of being, just as she found them along the way, showing them the signposts they need to conquer their demons in just the same way…I am wondering if I can really give a sense of her struggles and her triumphs and what you need to know……….

Now I wonder if you recognise this woman I know and when you think of all you have achieved, this current hurdle is a doddle, surely it is for this woman I know, for you know to move forward to where you want to be, oh! woman I know…this woman the healer, the entertainer, the cook and the friend, the hard worker, the campaigner and a fighter, I guess this woman I know....can deal with this thing that worries her and stalls her as it is such a small thing compared to all that has gone before...oh! woman I know.....

Example Story telling two

I want to tell you a story about a woman I know who is one of those people who always rises like a phoenix from the flames when trouble comes her way, as she has this determination to survive, the courage to find a way and make the best of any situation, now when I think about this woman I know, I think about her strength and her determination...

When she was a young girl her parents lost their business and she was torn away from her familiar world and ended up in a new place, with a new lifestyle nothing like the one she left behind, but this is where it began that resourcefulness and adaptability I know and see when I think of this woman I know, she made new friends, carved out a new life and tried to support her family in this change and it was a change that followed her from this early experience, when she was a young married woman, with a husband working hard and they were stuck in a rented house she was not prepared to stay, to stay in a place that was not right for them, she saw what happened with her parents and was determined to find her way out, so she trained as a secretary with a view to getting a job with a building society, so that she could get a cheap mortgage with no deposit and begin the journey that would provide a home for the family, she did not sit around and wait for something to happen, this woman I know, she made it happen because that is the kind of woman she is, this woman I know, when she has a dream, she will follow that dream, later in her life she wanted to move to France to have a good lifestyle in the country enjoying the food and the wine and she looked for a house, sold up and she was on her way, she wanted it to happen and did not sit around talking about it, but made it happen yet again. She is a survivor she is, and she makes things happen oh yes, a catalyst and energy that will not stay supressed. There have been times when it has been really tough, when her husband lost his job and she had to do two jobs herself, but she is a survivor and she will always find a way forward that is just the kind of person she is....

She has the ability to see an opportunity to see when things are about to change and she found herself working in Independent Broadcasting just as computers were taking over the scene and she watched and learned and got in on computers when they were just taking off and developed new skills to bring to the table, leading to jobs in companies with operations all over the world, just by watching and learning and seeing the lay of the land, an opportunity a way forward, she will see it and chase it because that is the kind of woman she is, this woman I know.

Did I mention how she loves to cook? And what a brilliant cook, she loves to be a host and gather people around her and entertain, nurture, make people feel welcome and have fun, in fact fun is something I think of when I think of her, there is a sense of fun around her, she creates and sparks into life and I can hear her laughter as it infects those around her and carries them with her, a host and entertainer, a nurturer, yes that is the kind of woman she is, this woman I know.

Now if you were to ask her one of her greatest strengths I think she would say the relationship to her grand kids, as she has made special time for them, she gives them quality time with her, each on their own and sometimes together as she encourages their inquisitive minds. They love being with their Grandma, they feel her energy and her fun and they are happy to go away on their own with her for adventures, she has encouraged them with reading and all their interests in their inquisitive young minds, the nurturer I guess, in this woman I know, her two girls first and so proud of them she is, one with her MA and her burgeoning career and the other so confident and smart with so many friends and with her two boys, growing fast and enjoying their travels with their grandma who opens up new vistas to their young minds, she so treasures this connection with her grandsons this woman I know, so proud of all her family and she likes to bring them all together if she can once a year, so they feel that bond and that connection, all are there for one another, family is important to her, all-important to her, this woman I am telling you all about today

What about her life as a therapist, I guess that just follows on, she receives such joy from her family she wanted to help others experience what she has experienced, so she began to specialise in fertility enhancement through therapy and she has helped so many women become Mums like her, giving them this chance for something they long for, some had been trying for years, some at the "last chance saloon" on their final round of IVF, 15 years of work helping woman to conceive, now how many young lives are now there, families flourishing, lives enhanced through her passion for her healing and her determination to help, that is the kind of woman she is, a healer and a nurturer, nurturing the dreams of people who have lost hope and returning that hope to them and helping them to succeed when they thought it was too late...

So what more can I tell you, she is a mother and a grandmother, a therapist and a friend, a businesswoman and an inspiration and a survivor too, an innovator and an anchor, a nurturer and a chef, there is nothing that can keep her down, surely given the story of this woman I know, can you see all you have done and all that you are, nothing now can hold you back, nothing can halt this story, this story of courage and progress and change but with fun and adventure along the way, you can do it now....you can achieve it now....that's right, oh woman I know.

Sample Sessions using material from the book

There are some sample sessions here to help you construct your self-hypnosis, they can be adapted to different areas and once you understand the structure it will make it easy for you to plan your work. Remember the planning is part of the therapy.

Simple Sample session with cue words for confidence

I am going to use the cue word blue for this exercise that you can copy.

Blue, say this and close your eyes and take your focus into your body.

Now give all your attention to your head..... aware of the muscles in your face that do so much work for you....communicating your feelings through your expression, allow the muscles to loosen as you give them attention and move away from your head down into your neck.... your head is often packed full of chasing thoughts so we want to move down into the body......you may have done a body scan in meditation before and that is similar to what we are doing now..... taking your attention down through your shoulders...... your arms into your hands.....into your fingers and thumbs.... just noticing as you go, just giving each part of your body that you visit your full attention for a moment....not for long...... it does not need to feel like a torturous slow exercise.....but just flowing through your body, down your back into your pelvis and noticing..... moving down your chest into your abdomen, moving through to the tops of your legs and then following this flow of attention, loosening those muscles as you go, down your legs into your feet, noticing any sensations there, any feeling on the soles of the feet.......and as you reach your feet, I wonder if you can notice which foot is most relaxed right now......that's right....... feeling in your toes and when you have completed this journey through your body, now tell yourself you have reached a place of stillness ready to do the work....

Say to yourself the word **Blue** again.

Now repeat the direct suggestions you need like:

I am confident and in control, I have all the skills I need in this situation.

I am full to the brim with confidence.

I am confident in all and every situation I encounter.

I am confident and in control, I have all the skills I need in this situation.

I am full to the brim with confidence.

I am confident in all and every situation I encounter.

I am confident and in control, I have all the skills I need in this situation.

I am full to the brim with confidence.

I am confident in all and every situation I encounter.

I am confident and in control, I have all the skills I need in this situation.

I am full to the brim with confidence.

I am confident in all and every situation I encounter.

Now say the word **Blue** and you will end this session.

You can use this simple process to tackle any issues, just decide on the direct suggestions you want to give to your subconscious.

Sample session for overthinking (can be done with or without recording)

Once you have settled yourself into a comfortable position, a quiet place where you will not be disturbed, once you have read this through, close your eyes and begin to allow your mind to focus in on your body for a moment and then come into your mind and imagine, see in your mind's-eye you are picking up a small note book/note pad..... when you open it you see the number 100 on the page in front of you.... nothing else.... just 100.... I want you to tear out that page and you will see underneath it has 99 written on it....... I would like you to tear that out revealing 98 below..... as you concentrate on the numbers and tearing each page out once the number is revealed you find yourself feeling surprisingly relaxed.......... perhaps hearing the sound of the page as it tears........ aware of the texture of the paper in your hand....... watching the numbers go down and down........ one page after another revealing the number below....... it is like opening Russian dolls and seeing the dolls get smaller and smaller........the numbers are getting smaller and smaller........ as the numbers get smaller and smaller you relax deeper and deeper........I wonder if you can notice how deeply you relax, as the numbers gets smaller and smaller........ as the number of torn pages grows the written numbers get smaller and you go deeper and deeper. Page after page.........the numbers descending like going down in a lift........ down and down........ focusing all of your attention on the numbers as they go down and down and take you into trance........ allowing yourself to drift right down into trance........ that's right so you can do the work you want to do today.......when the pad is empty........ the numbers all gone you will be in a comfortable trance........ all the numbers gone now until you need them again........ they will always be there for you to take you down, each time you practice this it will get easier and easier to go deeper and deeper into trance now.

Imagine you are visiting your mind for a moment...just a visitor... for a moment.......you see images flashing across a screen....the screen in your mind.....that's what it feels like....watching a story unfold......but is that what it feels like for you?.....sometimes.... just stepping back from those thoughts for a moment....and watching.....watching what happened yesterday.......imagining what might happen tomorrow...rehearsing a conversation...

around and around it goes...fragments of speech....words...ideas....all flashing by...stream of consciousness they call it.......and a stream it is indeed........on and on it flows...sometimes it feels like you cannot keep up with it....you can get swept away with it....with no reality check at all....is this really what I think?....Is this really what I feel? ....Where am I in all this stuff?...these flashing images....dialogues.......ideas.......

But they are all up there in your mind....busy.....busy....busy...all flashing past on the screen...but it is just a screen...so if it is a screen with projections on.......like the old projector at the cinema.......do we have to keep watching........do we have to keep listening.....if we do not like what we see....if we do not like what we hear.....stop.......stop watching that screen......stop listening to the dialogue.....it is time to switch it off....find a different story.....a new film......a better film......one that makes you feel good instead of bad....you are the watcher....the observer......so step back in your mind and decide........what do you want to watch.....you might even hear my voice in your head from time to time....reminding you.......you are the watcher.....watching the thoughts on the screen.......and as a watcher....an observer........you can choose to stop....do I want to watch this one............or shall I fast forward to the next......move on......move on to a new story........

Every day I change my mind about things........ I change it about whether I want a tea or a coffee....... do I turn left or right.......which way to go, which way to turn........ what can I find now that will help me back on track...........making those chemicals in my brain spark it back into life again......... using my imagination to create the thoughts that send those endorphins into my mind.....or maybe go for a run........ lift some weights or swim........ I can think about the things that will push my mind into a different place and choose to push it there, taking control again........ not free-falling but seeing those chemical levels rise...... serotonin increasing, I am making it increase, I have read

SAMPLE SESSIONS USING MATERIAL FROM THE BOOK

about the placebo and the nocebo, so which will it be, using the power of my mind to choose the positive thoughts...... making those chemicals rise, I can do it, I can, I can...

And now I am going to awaken again, it is time again to come around again and I am going to use those numbers to bring me back, but just five of them and when I reach the count of five I will wake up....1.............2.............3...........4...........5.........I am awake now.

A more complex sample session for recording, focusing on anger

Remember, when you are recording speak slowly and perhaps imagine you are reading a bedtime story to a child, keeping your voice soft and relaxed.

Just imagine that you are in a car..... a simple visualisation just for now..... you are in the car and it is raining.....but you are not driving this car..... you are being driven..... so you can relax back in the passenger seat and go along for the ride..... the rain is hitting the windscreen.... so the windscreen wipers are on.......... imagining this now and making the image even clearer, seeing the windscreen wipers moving from side to side........ sweeping back and forth, back and forth........ you may find yourself watching those wipers as they move back and forth...... back and forth and you can easily create this image in your mind...... when you want to slip into trance to do some work for you......... watching that steady movement back and forth, you might even find yourself moving and swaying with that rhythm, but noticing even more detail now......... in this rainy scene....... driving along in the car....... the rain is hitting the windscreen and you can see the splats of water hitting the screen and drizzling down......... running down the glass and then the wipers come along and sweep it away and then it starts again........ more rain again........ hitting the windscreen and beginning its journey down the glass and now hearing that rain as it hits the glass, that pattering sound of the rain smattering........... pattering against the glass as you drift deeper into trance and the wipers may make a sound too..... most wipers do...... that swiping..... wiping sound moving across the glass.... swish...... swish...... the sounds anchoring you there in the image and the clear goblets of water hitting the screen and you seeing it there and then there is the back and forth, back and forth as the wipers keep the windscreen clear......so you can see the road up ahead....... but what matters right now is seeing this scene in your mind and allowing trance to occur..... only when you see this in your mind, this journey in your mind, taking you into trance, drifting into that quiet space where you can do the work you want to do for you, that's right....... Now count down from 10 – 1 following the numbers down as if you were going down steps 10..........9...............8..................7.................6 drifting down now............5............4.........relaxing deeper now................3................2 nearly there and 1, very deeply relaxed now.

Perhaps I could think about a fire now....A fire starts from a spark.... a spark that has to be fanned and encouraged to survive..... I wonder if you have ever seen fire start in the old fashioned way by rubbing two sticks together.... the smoke rises,.....then there is the spark which you blow upon to sustain it...... then feed it with materials that will burn and it will burst into fire...... real fire not just a spark......but you have to keep fanning the flames, encouraging them......... you have to keep feeding the fire to keep it alight and it needs oxygen to survive........... so many things in place to keep the fire burning... ....I would like to suggest to you that your anger is just like that fire........ starting from a small spark...... a flare of anger....... but you have to sustain that anger to keep it there.....fan it with your attention..... feeding it with new reasons..... new ideas of why it is justified......why you have a right to feel it....... all that self-justification for your anger..... feeding it and making it flare.... of course you have the choice to remove your attention from it and stop fanning the flames of it.......... stop nursing that anger into life........ stop coaxing that anger into existence. I wonder if you can catch it when it is just a spark......... just beginning........ or whether it will have truly caught before you stop the anger........ before you withdraw your attention from it and it fizzles out and I wonder if you have noticed when you have left that anger behind........ there are times in the past when you have known that feeling........ that angry feeling and now you know that feeling has passed...... it is in the past and how you cannot reignite it...... in fact sometimes it is hard to remember just how you managed to create such a massive fire from such a small spark..... but now you know you have snuffed it out....... you could even imagine...... more than withdrawing your attention and no longer fanning the flames of it, you could see yourself throwing a bucket of water over it and completely snuffing it out...... best way to be sure....... to be sure of leaving it in the past where it belongs..... I wonder when you will notice that moment has passed....... right away or a few minutes from now........ that you notice the fire has gone out.

What purpose does this anger have for me right now? what is it doing for me? maybe it feels it is protecting me....... if it is protecting me.......what is it protecting me from? Why do I need protecting? Is my anger the best way to protect me in this situation?........ Can I find another way to protect myself in this situation? Am I in any real danger?........ Or is this just perceived danger?....... What else can do for me what my anger has been doing for me but is not going to do now, as I have decided I can find better ways to achieve this?

My anger does not just hurt others but it hurts me too and I no longer want to do things that hurt me, I want to protect me and the best way to protect me is to find another way to protect me and leave the anger in the past, behind me in the past with the other things I used to do, but do not do any more as they are hurtful to me. I am free from anger now, it is a past part of me, I leave this part of me in the past, how good it feels to know I do not need this anger any more, what an incredible relief.....

I wonder if I try not to notice when that anger just snuffs out like a candle guttering out when your back is turned…….. just snuffed out without me noticing that the moment has passed and that a calm peace is returning to me………… the firework lying spent on the ground, the moment has passed………I wonder if I can notice how calm I feel now, or do I need to notice or just enjoy the moment of calm I feel right now.

And now it is time to awaken again, I have done some good work today, sown the seeds of change today deep in my mind today, so that I can feel calmer than before, so I can awaken now and I will count back up from the numbers I followed down, all the way up from 1 to 10……..1…………2……….3………..gradually following the numbers up………..4………..5…………….6…….getting more awake now………….7…………..8…………….9………..10 that's right, wide awake.

www.ingramcontent.com/pod-product-compliance
Lightning Source LLC
Chambersburg PA
CBHW051650040426
42446CB00009B/1071